George Washington

America's Leader in War and Peace

Leaders of the American Revolution

Leaders of the American Revolution

George Washington
America's Leader in War and Peace

Tim McNeese

CHELSEA HOUSE
PUBLISHERS
A Haights Cross Communications Company ®
Philadelphia

CHELSEA HOUSE PUBLISHERS
VP, NEW PRODUCT DEVELOPMENT Sally Cheney
DIRECTOR OF PRODUCTION Kim Shinners
CREATIVE MANAGER Takeshi Takahashi
MANUFACTURING MANAGER Diann Grasse

Staff for George Washington
EXECUTIVE EDITOR Lee Marcott
EDITORIAL ASSISTANT Carla Greenberg
PRODUCTION EDITOR Noelle Nardone
PHOTO EDITOR Sarah Bloom
COVER AND INTERIOR DESIGNER Keith Trego
LAYOUT 21st Century Publishing and Communications, Inc.

First Printing

9 8 7 6 5 4 3 2 1

Library of Congress Cataloging-in-Publication Data

McNeese, Tim.
  George Washington: America's leader in war and peace/Tim McNeese.
    p. cm.—(Leaders of the American Revolution)
  Includes bibliographical references and index.
  ISBN 0-7910-8619-4 (hardcover)
  1. Washington, George, 1732–1799—Juvenile literature. 2. Presidents—
United States—Biography—Juvenile literature. I. Title. II. Series.
E312.66.M35. 2005
973.4'1'092—dc22

                                    2005002093

All links and web addresses were checked and verified to be correct at the time of publication.
Because of the dynamic nature of the web, some addresses and links may have changed since
publication and may no longer be valid.

Contents

The Early
Years

More than 200 years after his death, George Washington remains one of the most important men in American history. We see his image on the quarter and the dollar bill, and his name marks locations throughout our country. Each site, building, company, bridge, or street that features the first president's name helps to keep his memory alive and honors the man who played such a critical role in the creation of the United States of America. Towns and counties named after the great patriot leader are found in nearly every state. Even the nation's capital bears his name.

In the heartland of America, the first president shares a place on the side of Mount Rushmore in the Black Hills of South Dakota with three other great presidents—Thomas Jefferson, Abraham Lincoln, and Theodore Roosevelt. A great statue of Washington's head has been carved out of solid granite, measuring six stories tall from his chin to the top of his head. In the Black Hills, George Washington's place in the history of the United States is forever carved in stone.

But while George Washington remains an important figure in America's past, much of what we know of his life is based on myths and legends—stories of the young Washington chopping down one of his father's cherry trees, or throwing a silver dollar across the mile-wide Potomac River. But these attempts to create a larger-than-life, mythic figure from our first president are unnecessary. The real George Washington was a man who lived and worked and wrote and fought alongside other men and women who wanted to create a better

George Washington is one of four presidents honored on Mount Rushmore in South Dakota. Washington's head (on the far left), carved out of granite, measures six stories from the chin to the top of the head.

world for themselves. His life was filled with adventure, drama, and success, as well as disappointment, discouragement, and failure. That Washington lived and helped to create a new nation based on democratic principles and ideals is no myth. And the story is as exciting as any found on the pages of American history.

YOUNG GEORGE WASHINGTON

George Washington was born on February 11, 1732, in a farmhouse on a bluff overlooking Pope's Creek in Virginia's Westmoreland County. Indians had lived at the site earlier, where they caught oysters in the river waters nearby. Over the years, these Native Americans created great piles of oyster shells. When the Indians abandoned the hillside and moved to another location, the place became known as Oyster Shell Hill.

At the time of Washington's birth, Virginia was one of 13 British colonies that hugged the eastern coast of North America. Washington's parents were Augustine and Mary Ball Washington, and his great-grandfather was a seaman named John Washington, who had sailed from England to America in 1657. It was John Washington who had first established the plantation on Oyster Shell Hill, which he called Wakefield Farm. Once in America, he had prospered and become a member of the Virginia House of Burgesses, which helped make the laws for the colony.

George Washington's father, Augustine, was born in 1694. Like the grandfather after whom he was named, Augustine Washington was a hard-working, fairly wealthy Virginian who also served in the House of Burgesses. He worked the lands he inherited at Pope's Creek, a stream that flowed into the Potomac River. Augustine also owned an ironworks, an important industry in early America. He operated a gristmill and, for a time, served as the local justice of the peace and sheriff.

Augustine Washington's first wife, Jane Butler Washington, died in 1729 while Augustine was away on a trip to England. Two years later, he married his second wife, Mary Ball, who was 15 years younger than Augustine. She became stepmother to Augustine's three children, and she and Augustine would have six more children of their own. George was the first, arriving 11 months after they married.

Little is known about George Washington's early years. This may explain why some well-meaning writers later made up stories about young George chopping down cherry trees and telling his father, "I cannot tell a lie." Some facts about Washington's childhood are known, however. Virginia in the 1730s was still a frontier colony, and George's father had to work hard, along with George's older half-brothers, to clear the family's lands, work the tobacco fields, and uproot the stumps of trees (none of them cherry trees) that Augustine himself actually did chop down. The Washingtons also owned black slaves who worked on Augustine's lands, tending the tobacco fields. The Washingtons and their neighbors still lived with Indians fairly close by, although young George did not see any of them during the first ten years of his life.

While George was still a boy, his father continued to add thousands of acres to the lands he owned. He purchased 2,500 acres from his sister—land that would one day be the location for Mount Vernon, George Washington's estate. But Augustine was never an extremely wealthy man. While George did not grow up poor, there were wealthier plantation owners who lived nearby, farmers who owned some of the best, most fertile lands in Virginia, as well as hundreds of slaves. The house George lived in until he was six years old had been built by his grandfather and was a rather shabby wooden building. There were not enough sheets for all the beds in the Washington home, and while the family's spoons were made of silver, the forks were carved from wood.

It was the discovery of iron ore on Augustine's property that helped to make the family a little more prosperous. In time, Augustine had enough money to afford to send both of George's half-brothers, Lawrence and Augustine, Jr., to school in England, where the sons of the best Virginia families were educated.

When George was six years old, he and his family moved to a new plantation, Ferry Farm, in King George County, on the banks of the Potomac River. The plantation specialized in the prized Virginia crop, tobacco. Tobacco prices were usually good, and the harvested tobacco leaves were shipped to England. The money made from tobacco sales helped provide the Washington family with the things they needed, including tools, furniture, clothing, and books.

YEARS OF LEARNING

Like most young colonial children, George first learned at home, where his mother taught him his ABCs. Later, a local churchman named Mr. Hobby instructed him in reading, writing, and simple arithmetic problems. Spelling was a problem for Washington. Even as an adult, he had trouble remembering the correct spelling of such words as "pierce," "ceiling," and "seize." Mathematics was his favorite subject, and young Washington later learned trigonometry, which helped him in his first profession—surveyor.

George kept a *Copy Book* in which he wrote important things he wanted to remember. Always a polite young man, he reminded himself in his notebook to: "Cleanse not your teeth with the tablecloth," "In the presence of others sing not to yourself nor drum with your fingers or feet," "Kill no vermin, fleas, lice, or ticks in the sight of others."[1]

George's official schooling probably lasted only until the young boy was about eleven years old. That same year, 1743, George's father died. George received the news while visiting some of his cousins on another plantation. It was spring, and young Washington was busy participating in games and playing cards with his younger relatives. While there, he also enjoyed two of his favorite pastimes: horse-back riding and fox hunting.

When he received the news about his father, Washington rode home as soon as he could. His father's death greatly saddened the young boy. In Augustine's will, he gave most of his 10,000 acres of land to George's two older half-brothers. As for George, he was to receive Ferry Farm, some additional land, and ten slaves when he turned 21 years of age. Until then, he was to live with his mother.

George's mother loved her son, but she was a difficult woman in many ways. She was extremely protective of him and did not want him far from her at any time. She could sometimes be harsh with her children, including George. There were times when she nagged her son and complained often that she had been abandoned by her husband to take care of a house full of children on her own. As a result, he and his mother did not have a warm, close relationship.

While young George was never very close to his mother, he held a great affection and admiration for his half-brother, Lawrence. Lawrence Washington was 14 years older than George, and attended school in England during George's early years. When he returned to Virginia, Lawrence treated George kindly and gave him personal attention. He sparked the imagination of his younger brother by telling him stories of his days on the high seas and of his war experiences fighting the Spanish under the command of Admiral Edward Vernon. (It was Lawrence who named the family farm Mount Vernon, after his naval commander.) When George decided that he wanted to

Washington's half-brother, Lawrence, was the first owner of Mount Vernon, which he inherited upon the death of their father in 1743.

join the British Navy, Lawrence was very supportive. But Mrs. Washington refused to allow her teenage son to become a sailor.

Through Lawrence, George was introduced to the most important people in Virginia society. In 1743, Lawrence married Anne Fairfax, the daughter of

Colonel William Fairfax, an important man in Virginia and one of the wealthiest men in all of the 13 colonies. A portion of Fairfax's vast land holdings bordered the Washington farm, and through his new sister-in-law, George was introduced to a colonial society of great wealth, prestige, and political power. He attended formal dinners and dances, and witnessed an elegant lifestyle that he both admired and envied.

Fairfax also owned a large library of books and allowed George to read any of them that he wanted. Through the Fairfax family, George became fully aware that there was more to life—more opportunities, more privileges, and greater wealth—than what he had previously experienced. But the influence of the Fairfax family did not immediately spring George into a world of glamour and luxury. Instead, it first led him to the challenging and dangerous Virginia frontier.

Test Your Knowledge

I   Where does George Washington's image appear?
   a. On the dollar bill.
   b. On the quarter.
   c. On Mount Rushmore.
   d. All of the above.

2   Where was George Washington born?
   a. In Brighton, England.
   b. In Philadelphia, Pennsylvania.
   c. In Westmoreland County, Virginia.
   d. In Potomac, Maryland.

3   Where was George Washington educated?
   a. In England.
   b. At the College of William and Mary in Williamsburg.
   c. At his home and at the home of a local churchman.
   d. At Harvard College.

4   Why was the Washington home named Mount Vernon?
   a. Vernon was the name of George Washington's grandfather.
   b. Vernon was the name of Lawrence Washington's naval commander.
   c. "Vernon" is a type of tobacco grown in the region.
   d. It was named for the green hills surrounding the home.

5 What happened when George Washington wanted to enlist in the British Navy?

a. His mother refused to allow him to leave home.

b. His half-brothers refused to help him.

c. The British Navy rejected his application because he was a colonist.

d. The Fairfax family urged him to join the Virginia militia instead.

ANSWERS: 1. d; 2. c; 3. c; 4. b; 5. a

Coming of Age

In 1748, George Washington began what would become one of the most exciting years of his life. He was 16 years old, and at more than six feet tall he was far taller than most of the men he met. Outdoor work on his father's farm had turned him into a well-built, strong-looking individual, his skin darkened by the sun. His dark hair framed an awkward-looking face, with deep blue eyes spaced widely apart, high cheekbones, a wide forehead, and a jaw that failed to hide young Washington's bad teeth. His hands were, as his French friend during the American Revolution, Lafayette, later described them, the largest "ever seen in a human being."[2] His feet were also quite large, requiring a size 13 shoe.

By 1748, Washington was spending much of his time living at Mount Vernon, Lawrence's Potomac home. Through Lawrence's wife, George learned the more refined skills of society, including the art of dancing and of making polite conversation. Outdoors, he spent time hunting, fishing, and horseback riding.

But Washington needed to find a profession, and with his natural mathematics skills, he developed a strong interest in surveying. In fact, he taught himself many of the skills needed for surveying. Lawrence encouraged George's interest in surveying by asking him to accurately measure his large turnip fields. The drawing young Washington made still exists today.

Measuring turnip fields was only the beginning. Through his connections with the Fairfax family, George was hired that spring to join a small group of surveyors enlisted by Colonel Fairfax to survey his

Washington spent most of his teen years living with Lawrence at Mount Vernon, where he began to develop an interest in surveying.

lands. Fairfax owned so much property that he was not certain where its borders were. His land included more than five million acres of Virginia frontier wilderness lying to the west.

The surveying party was led by James Genn, an older, experienced land surveyor. Washington was not yet qualified to assist with the surveying, but Lawrence suggested that he accompany the party to watch the real surveyors at their work and to serve as a companion to Colonel Fairfax's son, George William, who was seven years older than Washington.

AN ADVENTURE IN THE WILDERNESS

The surveying party set out for the Virginia mountains to the east on the morning of March 11, 1748. By the second day, they had reached the Shenandoah River. Washington kept a brief journal and wrote down his experiences and observations. While the surveying trip to the wilderness had its exciting moments, Washington sometimes summed up a day with a simple phrase: "Nothing Remarkable happened."[3]

The lands through which the surveyors traveled were rugged and mostly uninhabited. The party frequently slept outdoors under the stars. One night, heavy rains and wind blew the surveyors' tent over, soaking the group. On another night, a spark from the campfire set Washington's straw bed on fire. Sometimes the party reached a cabin, where a settler might let them

From Colonies to the Frontier

For nearly a century and a half, European colonists and their descendents established the British colonies of North America along the Atlantic coast. During those decades, from the early 1600s to 1750, colonists moved fewer than 100 miles up the various rivers that flowed out of the western Appalachian Mountains into the Atlantic. But by the second half of the eighteenth century, adventurous colonists were migrating west to the mountains and beyond into a new type of frontier. It was into this region that young Washington ventured in the late 1740s as a surveyor.

Within a few short years, the way west into Kentucky, Ohio, and Tennessee was clearly established by the backwoodsmen and frontiersmen. Those pioneers included such famous explorers and settlers as Daniel Boone. But Boone was not the first to explore these territories.

In 1750, Dr. Thomas Walker was appointed agent for the Loyal Land Company of Virginia, which had acquired a land grant of 800,000 acres two years earlier. Walker was sent to explore the Virginia wilderness for settlement. After traveling a month through the uncharted regions of Virginia, he and his fellow explorers reached

"Cave Gap," which Walker, a few days later, renamed "Cumberland Gap."

This entry route through the Appalachians into Kentucky would be used by thousands of pioneers in the years that followed. Close behind Walker came Christopher Gist, who explored nearly all of Kentucky as far as the Miami River. In 1752, another explorer, John Finley, reached the site of the Falls of the Ohio River near modern-day Louisville, Kentucky.

Three years later, the paths of Finley and Daniel Boone crossed. That summer, both Finley and Boone participated in a march into the wilderness of western Pennsylvania led by a British general, Edward Braddock. Boone was a colonial wagon teamster on the military campaign. During the march, Finley told Boone stories of the great hunting to be had in Kentucky. Boone became so inspired by Finley's stories of a hunter's paradise west of the Appalachians that he became determined to see Kentucky for himself. Although there is no historical record that he ever met directly either Boone or Finley, another officer was in command of Virginia troops on Braddock's march—young George Washington.

sleep overnight. At one inn, Washington was given a thin blanket, which he later found to be filled with "Vermin such as Lice [and] Fleas."[4]

The surveying trip became a way for Washington to learn how to live in the wilderness. He lived outdoors and suffered the difficulties of the trail. He slept in wet clothes and cooked wild game over an open fire. He tried his hand at hunting wild turkeys, but his aim with a rifle was poor, causing some of the older men to poke fun at him. On one occasion, he and William Fairfax became lost in the woods. But Washington did serve the surveying party well. For example, he knew the names of many of the trees the group encountered while surveying. This was important, since many of the boundary lines the surveyors created were marked by the local trees—hickory, ash, walnut, and sugar maple.

Washington experienced the same difficulties as the rest of the surveying party. The trails they used were hard to follow, sometimes no more than old Indian paths. Heavy rains made trails slippery for the horses. The men had to make difficult and dangerous river crossings. Indians lived on some of the lands the party surveyed, and the men kept a watchful eye. In fact, Washington and the surveyors did meet Indians on one occasion at the end of their second week in the wilderness. But the meeting went well.

The group of Virginians had camped at a trading post near Oldtown, Maryland. As the men rested, Washington cleaned his clothes. Suddenly, a party of 30 Indians walked into their campsite. The warriors were returning from a raid against another Indian tribe. Washington saw a scalp hanging from a warrior's belt. The Indian men were disappointed that they had not taken more Indian scalps.

Almost immediately, the surveyors and the warriors turned the meeting into a party. The Indians were given some rum and soon they were performing a war dance about the campfire. Washington was delighted by the evening's festivities. In his journal, he wrote how one warrior "jumps up as one awaked out of a Sleep & Runs & Jumps about the Ring in a most [comical] manner."[5] Washington even described how the Indians made music from a water-filled pot, which they used as a drum, and "a [Gourd] with some Shott in it to Rattle."[6]

After nearly five weeks in the woods of the Virginia wilderness, William Fairfax and George Washington left the surveyors and returned to Belvoir, the Fairfax estate. They reported to Colonel Fairfax about their adventures on the frontier and the work of the surveyors. By April 13, young Washington thankfully wrote in his journal: "Mr. Fairfax got safe home and I myself safe to my Brothers which concludes my Journal."[7]

Washington's work with the surveying party did not go unrewarded. Not only did he receive good pay for his month's work, but Fairfax was so pleased with Washington's efforts that he helped him become the surveyor of Culpeper County the following year. George Washington was only 17 years old. In his new role as surveyor, Washington helped lay out the site for a new town: Alexandria, Virginia. The small community was built close to the site where a great American city would one day exist, named for Washington himself.

Test Your Knowledge

1 What was George Washington's first profession?

   a. Sailor.

   b. Farmer.

   c. Surveyor.

   d. Teacher.

2 How did his half-brother encourage George Washington's interest in surveying?

   a. By asking him to measure his turnip fields.

   b. By asking him to measure his tobacco fields.

   c. By asking him to measure the woods behind Mount Vernon.

   d. By giving him a book on surveying.

3 Where did Washington's first surveying expedition take him?

   a. To the Virginia frontier wilderness.

   b. To determine the border between Virginia and North Carolina.

   c. To the colony's capital in Williamsburg.

   d. To the Ohio territory.

4 What happened when a party of Indians walked into the campsite of the surveyors?

   a. The Indians attacked the surveyors.

   b. The meeting turned into a party.

   c. The surveyors offered to measure the cornfields of the Indians.

   d. The surveyors agreed to leave their campsite immediately.

5 Which city did George Washington help to lay out as surveyor of Culpeper County?

   a. Annapolis, Maryland.

   b. Roanoke, Virginia.

   c. Norfolk, Virginia.

   d. Alexandria, Virginia.

ANSWERS: 1. c; 2. a; 3. a; 4. b; 5. d

Conflicts in the Wilderness

ashington's work as a surveyor helped him establish his first career. From the money he earned, he began to purchase his own land. In colonial Virginia, wealth was often measured by how much property one owned. By age 18, Washington claimed nearly 1,500 acres on the lower Shenandoah River, and over the next few years, he acquired more. By the time he was 25 years old, Washington owned some 4,000 acres. Tragically, some of that land had been inherited from his half-brother Lawrence following his unfortunate death.

Lawrence had become sick in the late 1740s, suffering from tuberculosis, which seriously damages a person's ability to breathe due to lung infection. Treatment options for the disease did not exist in the eighteenth century, and in 1751, Lawrence decided to visit the West Indies, hoping that the salt sea air might help him recover. George went with his brother to the Caribbean island of Barbados. The trip by ship made George quite seasick. It would also be the only time he ever traveled beyond American soil. In the island port of Bridgetown, the two brothers lived in an exotic world of sandy beaches, a busy harbor, and colorful tropical birds and palm trees. But the trip did not improve Lawrence's health. George, in fact, became ill himself. He struggled with smallpox for several weeks—a disease that was fatal for many colonists— but George survived. The two men returned to Virginia, where Lawrence died during the summer of 1752.

Lawrence's death was a crushing blow to George. That same year, Lawrence's only surviving child, a daughter, died two months after her father. On her death, Washington inherited Lawrence's estate.

AN EXPEDITION INTO THE UNKNOWN

It was a time of personal tragedy for Washington, and a time of crisis for his homeland. A clash between the English and French in North America was brewing. While the British had established 13 colonies along the coast of the Atlantic Ocean during the 1600s and early 1700s, the French had extended their authority over Canada to the north. However, both countries claimed some of the same territory. The lands to the west— people generally called this uncharted territory "The Ohio Country"—became a place of conflict between the two European powers. The territory in question included parts of western New York and Pennsylvania, as well as the lands bordered on the north by the Great Lakes and on the south by the Ohio River. (Much of this territory is today the states of Ohio, West Virginia, and Michigan.)

Until 1748, France and England had managed to avoid full-scale conflict over the Ohio Country. But that year a colonial land company, known as the Ohio Company, began selling land in the region. The

George Washington's Women

While still a teenager, George Washington began to learn a trade and gain experience on the frontier of Virginia. Washington was a serious young man, who had suffered the loss of his father when he was only 11 and had helped to support his family from a young age. But while he assumed great responsibility while still in his teens, he still found time for hunting, fishing—and girls.

Washington appears to have fallen in love several times, but little is known about these early love interests. In a letter he penned to a friend at age 17 or 18, he wrote about his "former passion" for a girl he described as a "Low Land Beauty."*

Washington also wrote poetry to those he admired. In one poem to a passing love interest named Frances Alexander, he used her name as the first letter of each line, writing:

> From your bright sparkling Eyes, I was undone;
> Rays, you have more transparent than the Sun,
> A midst its glory in the rising Day,
> None can you equal in your bright array;
> Constant in your calm and unspotted mind;
> Equal to all, but will to none Prove kind,
> So knowing, seldom one so Young, you'l Find.

One young woman made a more permanent impression on Washington. In late 1748, when Washington was 16, his friend, George William Fairfax, married a lovely girl named Sarah Cary (known as Sally). She became a constant presence at the nearby Fairfax estate, Belvoir, and a constant distraction for Washington.

For the rest of his life, Washington remained fascinated with Sally Fairfax. He wrote letters to her secretly and, in one, described her as an "amiable beauty," noteworthy for her "mirth, good humor, ease of mind—and what else?"** In a letter addressed to her and dated September 12, 1758, Washington noted, "I profess myself a Votary of Love."*** However, Washington most likely knew that he could not act on his feelings, since she was a married woman, and since Washington, himself, was engaged to the woman who would soon become his wife—Martha Dandridge Custis.

---

* Ralph K. Andrist, ed., *George Washington: A Biography in His Own Words* (New York: Newsweek, 1972), 26.

** Quoted in Tim McNeese, *History in the Making: Sources and Essays of America's Past, Volume I* (New York: American Heritage, 1994), 128.

*** Ibid.

company wanted to build a fort at the site where the Ohio River begins, on the frontier of western Pennsylvania. (Today, the city of Pittsburgh stands at this location.) However, scouts for the company discovered that the French were already building forts of their own in the region. Fort Presque Isle, on the southern shores of Lake Erie, and Fort Le Boeuf, located 12 miles away, were among the first in 1753. Others were planned for the following year. When the French began building forts in this disputed territory, British authorities responded.

By the fall of 1753, the Lieutenant Governor of Virginia, Robert Dinwiddie, received instructions from England to send a message to the French, informing them that they were building on English soil. The message also instructed them to leave the region. To deliver this letter to French authorities, Dinwiddie chose George Washington. (Dinwiddie had much at stake in these events, since he was one of the men who had organized the Ohio Company.) Washington was only 21 years old at the time, but he had experience along the frontier and had already been made a major in the Virginia colonial militia. Washington had actually volunteered for the mission to the French when he learned of Dinwiddie's plans.

Washington, as a 21-year-old major in the Virginia militia, was selected to carry a message to Fort Le Boeuf, ordering French troops to leave the Ohio Country.

By October 1753, Major Washington was on his way up the Potomac River with six companions, including a Dutchman who could speak French. The trip to Fort Le Boeuf and back took two and a half months. The journey was difficult. The weather was miserable, as rains swelled rivers until they "were quite impassible, without swimming our Horses."[8] The small party had to make many such river crossings. But the men finally reached Fort Le Boeuf, and Washington delivered his message. In response, the French politely informed him that they had no intention of leaving the Ohio Country, telling the young major, "it was their absolute Design to take possession of the Ohio, and, by God, they would do it."[9] Washington could do nothing but return and report to Dinwiddie.

The return trip proved even more difficult. It was winter, and the cold caused rivers to partially freeze. During one crossing, Washington was knocked off the raft on which he was riding and nearly drowned. The party encountered Indians, who fired on them, narrowly missing Washington. But the young major proved himself a levelheaded leader.

A FRONTIER FIGHT

Dinwiddie was not satisfied with the French response. He soon sent Washington back into the Ohio Country frontier on a second mission. This time, the results would be very different. Instead of six companions, Washington had more than 150 men under his command. (Dinwiddie had promoted him to lieutenant colonel in the Virginia militia.) The force left for the Pennsylvania wilderness in April 1754. Their goal was a fort the French were building along the headwaters of the Ohio River—Fort Duquesne.

Washington's march went poorly. Many of his colonial troops were unenthusiastic about their mission, especially since they were poorly fed and underpaid. But Washington pressed on. Along the way, he encountered a group of Delaware Indians, led by their chief, Half-King. Washington had met Half-King during his mission to the French the previous fall. The warrior leader hated the French and even claimed that they had captured and killed his father years before. It was Half-King who informed Washington of a group of Frenchmen camped nearby. Washington, uncertain of what to do and fearing that they might attack his force, decided to use the element of surprise to his advantage and attack first.

Washington should not have attacked at all. The British and French were not officially at war. But the young officer was inexperienced and not yet tested in battle. On the morning of May 28, Washington and his men surprised the French encampment of nearly three dozen men, catching them off guard. According to Washington's report, the fight lasted little more than 15 minutes. Ten Frenchmen were killed and 21 were taken prisoner. At least one escaped. Among those killed was a Frenchman named Joseph Coulon, Sieur de Jumonville, whom Half-King dispatched with a blow to his head and then scalped. As for Washington's forces, only one man was killed.

The deaths of the surprised Frenchmen in the wilderness of western Pennsylvania should not have taken place. Those who were killed had already surrendered and been taken prisoner. Washington would have normally sent the prisoners back to the Virginia capital, Williamsburg. But Half-King and his warriors took events into their own hands and killed several of their captives before Washington could stop them. (When Washington did halt the deaths of the remaining captives, Half-King and his warriors became offended and abandoned him.) When he later reported to his superiors in Virginia the details of the frontier skirmish, they approved of his attack. However, the dawn engagement would eventually earn Washington a reputation as a villain in the eyes of the French and other leaders in Europe.

When the smoke of battle cleared, Washington had gained his first fighting experience. The young militia officer was thrilled by the excitement of the fight. He later wrote innocently about the skirmish: "I heard the bullets whistle, and, believe me, there is something charming in the sound."[10] For the moment, Washington followed his victory by continuing his march toward Fort Duquesne.

When he was approximately 60 miles from the fort, he ordered his men to make camp and begin constructing their own fort. During the following weeks, he was reinforced with another 180 Virginia militiamen, and then 100 British Regular troops. But before the fortification was complete, the French attacked Washington's outpost on July 3. This time, the battle did not turn out in his favor. His palisade (or defensive barricade), Fort Necessity, sat in a poor place and was awash with water from a recent rainstorm. The rains had also dampened much of the garrison's powder. By day's end, with 30 men killed and 70 wounded, Washington surrendered to the French. He and his men were ordered to evacuate Fort Necessity and return to Virginia the following day. It was the Fourth of July, 1754.

Test Your Knowledge

I What illness did George Washington contract when he was in Barbados?

   a. Tuberculosis.

   b. Smallpox.

   c. Influenza.

   d. Malaria.

2 How did George Washington become the owner of Mount Vernon?

   a. He inherited it from his father.

   b. He inherited it from his half-brother, Lawrence.

   c. He bought it from his neighbor, Colonel Fairfax.

   d. His mother gave it to him.

3 What message did Major Washington carry to French settlers in the "Ohio Country"?

   a. They were building forts on English territory and needed to abandon them immediately.

   b. Their forts would not withstand the harsh winters and they needed to be modified.

   c. Their support was needed to help settle the western frontier.

   d. England wanted their help in establishing trading posts along the Ohio River.

4 Washington's first experience in battle involved an attack against which people?

a. The British.

b. Delaware Indians.

c. The French.

d. German Hessians.

5 What was the result of the attack on Fort Necessity on July 4, 1754?

a. Colonial forces triumphed over British Regulars.

b. The battle ended in a draw.

c. The French were defeated.

d. Washington surrendered to the French.

ANSWERS: 1. b; 2. b; 3. a; 4. c; 5. d

War on
the Frontier

Washington's loss at Fort Necessity was a blow to the young commander. His 350 men were simply no match for the French, who outnumbered his force by two to one. When Washington surrendered, he was forced to sign a paper, written in French, which stated the terms of his surrender. Among the words included in the document was

Washington's agreement that the colonists would not try to build another fort at the site for a year. In addition, Washington was accused in the death of Jumonville, one of the Frenchmen who had been murdered by Half-King two months earlier. The French claimed that Jumonville had actually been on a diplomatic mission. In effect, Washington admitted, by signing the surrender, that he had killed a French ambassador. When the story was told in France and throughout Europe, Washington became famous for a great crime against the French.

Washington's actions contributed to the climate of suspicion and conflict between France and England that would eventually lead to war. It was Washington who, in his surprise attack in April 1754, fired the first shots of a North American conflict that would become known as the French and Indian War (1754–1763).

By the time the war was fully underway in 1755, George Washington had already taken off his militia uniform for what he thought would be the last time. He made this decision even though he had been advanced to the rank of colonel at age 22. He resigned his militia officer's commission in 1754 after his return from his loss in the wilderness. In addition to feeling personally

Washington's actions at Fort Necessity signaled the beginning of the French and Indian War. The conflict between England and France spread beyond the 13 colonies. This scene depicts the Battle of the Plains of Abraham in 1759, in which French and British troops clashed in Quebec, Canada.

responsible for the defeat, he was also upset by the low pay and mistreatment at the hands of the British military. The British War Office had decided that Washington's Virginia Regiment was to be split up into separate companies, each led by a captain. As a result, Washington's rank would have been reduced from colonel to captain.

In addition, it was announced that all colonial officers would have to take orders from all British Regular Army officers, even if a British officer's rank was lower than that of the colonial officer. Instead, Washington turned in his resignation to Dinwiddie.

For a while, Washington, now a civilian, concentrated on his farming. He had Lawrence's Mount Vernon estate to run, as well as other lands. (Ferry Farm, one of his father's estates, was to have become his property when he turned 21, but two years had passed, and his mother had not given him the land.) Washington had barely become the new "squire of Mount Vernon"[11] before he received word that a large British army was to arrive in Virginia under the command of General Edward Braddock. The British general was a seasoned veteran of several European campaigns. Braddock's force was to march into the wilderness Washington had crossed more than once, attack Fort Duquesne, and drive the French out of the region.

Despite having resigned his commission, Washington wrote to Braddock when he reached America, offering his services. Braddock, with no experience fighting in North America, accepted Washington's offer.

Braddock was a career soldier who had spent 45 years in the military, and British authorities put their hopes in him during the summer of 1755. He came to America with two regiments, and with the rank of commander-in-chief of all British forces in North America. Braddock's plan was to advance into the frontier wilderness toward Fort Duquesne. There he would engage the French and their Indian allies, defeat them in battle, then oversee the fall of the fort and the removal of the French from the Ohio Country. Braddock intended to fight his battle European-style, meaning that he would face the enemy by lining up his men in several ranks or lines, his men firing in volleys and advancing until they were close enough to fix bayonets on their muskets and storm the enemy lines.

Washington met Braddock and his British Regulars at Wills Creek, which is known today as Cumberland, Maryland. Braddock apparently liked Washington and soon invited him to join his staff as a volunteer aide-de-camp. He was given the rank of colonel, but that was strictly a courtesy on Braddock's part. The newly arrived British commander did not think much of American colonial militia in general, noting with disgust that "their slothful and languid disposition" made "them unfit for military service."[12] In fact, during the months that he was in America, Braddock was only impressed by two colonials—George Washington and Benjamin Franklin, then a well-known printer, inventor, and public supporter of the war.

SHOWDOWN ON THE FRONTIER

After Braddock had assembled his men at Fort Cumberland, he set out for Fort Duquesne in May. He wisely chose to follow the same trail Washington had established over the Appalachian Mountains the previous year on his own failed march. But the advance was painfully slow. Baggage wagons and lumbering cannons dragged the advance to a near standstill. Some days, Braddock's 2,400 men barely covered two miles of territory.

By early July, the advance column of Braddock's march was near the Forks of the Ohio River, where the Monongahela and Allegheny Rivers joined at its headwaters. On July 9, following a river crossing on the Monongahela, the British and colonial forces were attacked, surrounded by the sharp sounds of musket fire and the loud whoops of more than 600 Frenchmen and Indians hiding in the thick underbrush. Braddock's column was stretched along a narrow, winding trail, unable to take formation and fight in their usual manner. The battle that unfolded sent the British into a panic, and they fled back down the narrow Indian path toward their comrades, Indian warriors moving in fast behind them. Soon, Braddock's forces were bottled up along the trail, presenting easy targets for their French and Indian enemies.

The Grave of General Braddock

When French and Indian fighters attacked Braddock's advancing column on July 9, 1755, no one was more surprised by the outcome of the "Battle of the Wilderness" than Braddock. His plan to engage the French in a European-style battle never took place. His shock and disbelief at the ambush and the loss that he and his men experienced was overwhelming. Doctors who attended the wounded general noted that Braddock appeared to die as much from anxiety as from his actual bullet wounds.

Braddock died during the retreat, and his body was quickly placed in a grave and hidden by his men as they marched over the site. While the French and their Indian allies never discovered the burial site of the defeated and humiliated British general, the site did not remain hidden forever.

Washington moved his men off the trail and into the trees, which provided them with cover. Braddock, unfortunately, kept his men in the open, and tried to line them up for volley firing. The British commander fought desperately. Four horses were shot out from under him. British troops were cut down by the dozens. (In the confusion, some even fired on one another.) One of those shot was Braddock. Meanwhile, Washington

In the years that followed, the trail that Braddock's men carved through the thick tree growth of western Pennsylvania became a commonly used route through this frontier region. For nearly 30 years, Braddock's grave remained undisclosed. Then, in 1804, workers unearthed some human remains near the place where Braddock was probably buried. After they were completely exposed, the skeletal remains were moved out of the road to a small, nearby hill. There they remained, still unnoted and unnoticed, until 1913. That year, an official marker was placed at the reburial site. Today, along Interstate Highway 40, visitors may stop and tour the gravesite that is part of a small park included in Fort Necessity National Battlefield.

moved about the field of battle, keeping his cool despite his youth and inexperience. Two horses were shot out from under him. At least four musket balls ripped through his uniform coat.

The battle lasted for several hours. Once the wounded Braddock was removed to the rear of the action, the British began their full retreat, leaving the bodies of their comrades behind to be scalped by Indians. Washington helped organize the retreat. Several men stated they had not even seen a single Indian during the fight, "they had just heard their blood-curdling yells." [13]

When the casualties were counted, the British left behind 900 men, either dead or wounded. Braddock died three days after the battle, his body buried along the wagon road his men had hacked through the wilderness. His men tromped over his gravesite to conceal it from the enemy, then continued on their march toward eastern Pennsylvania. As for Washington, he was terribly disappointed in the outcome of the battle. He noted that Braddock's forces had "been beaten, most shamefully beaten, by a handful of Men who only intended to molest and disturb our March." [14] He was suffering from a fever and dysentery, yet managed to perform well when the shooting began. He was proud of his fellow colonials, including his Virginians, but had little praise for the British Regulars and their lack of resolve in the fight. As for Braddock, Washington wrote later, "Thus died a man, whose good and bad qualities were intimately blended."[15]

Test Your Knowledge

I Why did the French view Washington as a criminal following his defeat at Fort Necessity?

    a. He had attacked without firing a warning shot first.

    b. He had stolen French supplies and weapons before marching back to Virginia.

    c. He had unwittingly signed a document admitting that he had killed a French ambassador.

    d. He had signed a peace treaty with the French six months earlier.

2 Washington fired the first shots in which war?

    a. The Revolutionary War.

    b. The French and Indian War.

    c. The Thirty Years' War.

    d. The Crimean War.

3 Why did Washington resign his commission in 1754?

    a. He was too old to fight in the war.

    b. He felt guilty about his role in the death of Jumonville.

    c. His mother needed his help managing the family estate.

    d. He felt that the policies of the British War Office were unfair to colonial officers.

4 Why was Washington able to protect many of his men while Braddock's troops were being slaughtered?

   a. Washington moved his men off the trail and into the cover of the trees.

   b. Washington ordered his men to retreat as soon as the battle began.

   c. Washington's men had better weapons and were more skilled in battle.

   d. The French and Indians specifically targeted the British troops and ignored the colonial soldiers.

5 What did Washington learn from the performance of the British troops under Braddock?

   a. They lacked resolve in the fight and their European style of battle was not suited to the wilderness.

   b. They did not respect their officers and would not follow orders.

   c. They preferred life in the American colonies to the life they had known in England.

   d. They were poorly trained and lacked weapons and equipment to survive the harsh winters.

ANSWERS: 1. c; 2. b; 3. d; 4. a; 5. a

The Coming of Revolution

The first major battle of the French and Indian War had ended in a rout for the British and their colonial allies. Washington's disappointment after the battle continued. With Braddock dead, his second-in-command, Colonel Thomas Dunbar, destroyed his army's cannon and wagons, everything that would slow down the retreat back to

Fort Cumberland at Wills Creek. Within weeks, completely demoralized, Dunbar abandoned the fort and marched his British forces to Philadelphia, where they moved into winter quarters. Dunbar and his men were not willing to fight again until the following year. In the meantime, Washington was appointed as commander-in-chief of all Virginia militia. He took up his post at Fort Cumberland. There he was to protect the entire 400-mile Virginia frontier with only 700 men at his disposal.

It would be a difficult command. Washington received few supplies. Indians attacked along the frontier, raiding settlements and killing frontier families. Unable to stop such attacks, Washington was soon criticized by representatives of the Virginia House of Burgesses, which nearly caused him to resign his commission. But he remained at his post until the Indian attacks lessened in 1757.

Through 1758, the British suffered several severe losses in the French and Indian War, including Braddock's defeat. Eventually, the British forces began to find some success. During the spring of 1758, Washington joined another march into the wilderness of western Pennsylvania as the British headed again to Fort Duquesne. This time, British Regulars marched under the command of Brigadier General John Forbes. It would be Washington's fourth march into the region in five years. Had Forbes followed Braddock's Road, he would have reached Fort Duquesne fairly quickly. But Forbes decided to approach the French garrison from another direction, which required another road to be constructed. The Forbes campaign dragged on for months. The troops did not reach Fort Duquesne until November.

Washington's first sight of the fort was both a triumph and a disappointment. Before Forbes's army reached the enemy's frontier outpost, the French burned Duquesne to the ground. With the French fort eliminated, Washington decided that it was time to leave military service. He resigned his officer's commission and returned to civilian life. His loyal Virginia troops took Washington's resignation hard. His officers expressed their sorrow in a letter to their commander: "Where will [our unhappy country] meet a Man so experience'd in military Affairs? One so renown'd for Patriotism, Courage and Conduct?"[16] Washington would not put on another military uniform for 16 years.

A RETURN TO CIVILIAN LIFE

The year 1758 brought several important changes to Washington's plans for the future. He left his service in the Virginia militia, but was elected as a member of the Virginia House of Burgesses. Membership in this representative body was a sign of Washington's importance and his growing reputation in the colony. At 26 years old, George Washington was considered a man of status and a leader.

Another important change took place for Washington that year. During the spring, before joining the Forbes campaign, Washington had stopped at the home of a friend while on his way to the Virginia capital at Williamsburg. There, he met a young widow named Martha Dandridge Custis. Martha was one of the richest women in Virginia. Her former husband, Colonel Daniel Parke Custis, had left her in charge of a considerable estate, which included slaves, livestock, investments, funds, and more than 17,000 acres of property.

Washington wasted little time in courting Martha. He called on her by mid-March, and within a week had proposed to her. She accepted, and the couple was married on January 6, 1759, at Martha's plantation

Washington married Martha Dandridge Custis in January 1759.

home. Washington was not quite 27 years old; his wife was a few months older.

The Washingtons presented quite a physical contrast. George towered well over six feet in height, while Martha was quite short. According to some reports, she learned to grab her husband by the coat lapels and pull him down toward her when she wanted to make certain that he was paying attention to what she was saying. Martha, by all accounts, was a pretty woman, although a bit plump. Washington wrote of the woman who would be his wife for the next 40 years: "I believe I have settled with an amiable wife for the remainder of my life and hope to find in my retirement more happiness than I have ever found in a large and troubled world."[17]

Martha brought two children to their marriage: a four-year-old boy named John Parke, who was called "Jackie," and a daughter, two years younger, named Martha but referred to as "Patsy." (Patsy was also the name George used for his wife, Martha.) While George and Martha would never have children of their own, Washington treated Martha's children as his own son and daughter, and became quite fond of Patsy, who suffered from epilepsy. When she died at age 17, Washington was deeply saddened.

George Washington took his seat as a new member of the Virginia House of Burgesses on February 22. He also began work expanding the house at Mount Vernon to make room for his new family. He ordered workmen to add an additional story to the house that faced a broad lawn sloping down to touch the bank of the Potomac River.

Washington devoted himself wholly to what he called his "retirement" to Mount Vernon, spending happy times with his new family. He was always buying Jackie and Patsy new toys and other gifts. Their Mount Vernon home was the constant scene of social events. The Washingtons hosted many friends and family visitors for "meals, for weekends, to go boating, to hunt foxes, to play cards."[18] Washington had become an extremely sociable man who enjoyed company. His diary of the time shows multiple entries of hosting guests, such as: "Mrs. Possey and some young woman whose name was unknown to any body in this family [dined] here."[19] From 1768 to 1775, the Washingtons hosted more than 2,000 guests at Mount Vernon.

On Washington's estate, he raised crops of tobacco and such grains as alfalfa, wheat, and barley. Washington enjoyed breeding hunting dogs and racehorses, and

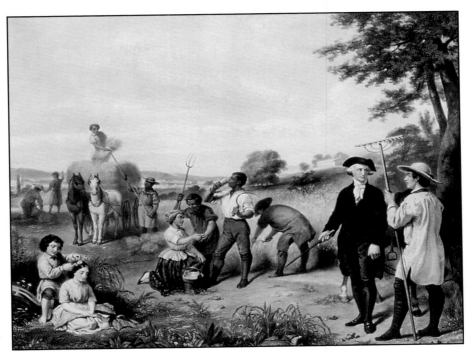

Washington enjoyed his brief "retirement" at Mount Vernon, spending time with his family, entertaining guests, experimenting with new farming techniques, and making plans to expand his home.

experimenting with new crops, such as hemp and flax. Such crops could be sold in the colonies easily, without having to be shipped to England, allowing him to avoid the high shipping rates of the period. He ordered books from London on the latest farming techniques. Washington even considered trying to raise bison, the wild animals that then roamed east of the Mississippi

River. While the experiment did not succeed, he continued to try; there was a buffalo cow at Mount Vernon in 1799, the year of his death.

Washington's public responsibilities also occupied his time. In addition to serving in the House of Burgesses, Washington became a county magistrate not long after his marriage. He also served as a church-warden, and joined several investment schemes, including land development companies, which failed to yield a profit. During the 1760s, Washington became a substantial citizen of Virginia. By age 40, in 1772, he ranked among the most powerful men in the colony.

COLONIAL PROTESTS BEGIN

As Washington enjoyed a quiet but busy "retirement," the world of the 13 American colonies was experiencing dramatic change. By 1763, the British had finally defeated the French in their Seven Years' War. Under the Treaty of Paris, the French were forced to abandon all their remaining claims to Canada, effectively removing them from power in North America. The disputed Ohio Country fell into British hands.

Despite winning the war, the British emerged from the international struggle having spent millions of pounds, doubling Britain's national debt to nearly 130 million pounds. While winning the French and Indian War was an important event for England, the country appeared to be teetering on the brink of bankruptcy.

Beginning in 1764 and for the next ten years, the British government implemented new customs duties and taxes on its colonies in North America to help pay for the cost of the war. Such acts of Parliament as the Currency Act, the Sugar Act, and the Stamp Act were extremely unpopular from Massachusetts to Georgia. As more and more colonists protested these actions by the British government, men like George Washington found themselves in the middle of a political tug-of-war between those who wished to remain loyal to England and others, calling themselves patriots, who wanted King George III and Parliament to leave them alone.

Washington's attitude toward Britain changed slowly. In 1765, when the British passed the Stamp Act, a law that required a tax to be paid for every colonial document—from newspapers to legal contracts to playing cards—protests erupted in nearly every colony, including Virginia. Washington left the more vocal protests to Patrick Henry, a fellow member of the

Washington's "Patowmack Canal"

During the 1760s and 1770s, more and more colonists were moving west of the Tidewater region toward the Appalachian Mountains in search of new lands and new homes. Many of those who moved inland followed the eastern-flowing rivers upstream, including the Potomac River. But rivers like the Potomac could be dangerous, due to rapids and waterfalls. The Great Falls and the Little Falls upriver from Georgetown, Maryland, kept pioneer migrants from using the Potomac for serious trade.

Washington decided that a series of short canals could be built to bypass these falls and create a safe water route. In 1772, he received permission to form a Potomac navigation company to build such canals. When the Revolutionary War began, Washington was forced to put off his plans for a Potomac Canal.

Once the war was over, Washington returned to his canal plans. He began campaigning for a man-made Potomac waterway. In 1785, both the Virginia and Maryland legislatures agreed to charter his venture, known as the Patowmack (the original spelling of the word "Potomac") Company.

Work began on the canal in the spring of 1786 at its southern and eastern ends. Two hundred workmen,

including immigrants and slaves, began construction at the Great Falls, upriver from Georgetown. Five locks were built to bypass the 77-foot drop in the river. Although the Great Falls locks were not completed until 1802 (three years after Washington's death), parts of the canal system began operating as early as 1788.

Although Washington had hoped to profit from the canal, he never saw much money from its operation. However, the northern and western terminus for the canal system was in Cumberland, Maryland, which became an important jumping-off place for western migrants. It was at Cumberland that an important western land route was begun—the National Road.

As for the canal, it remained in operation until 1830 when, having gone bankrupt, it was taken over by another canal company. During the 40 years it was in service as "Washington's Canal," the man-made waterway brought $10 million worth of goods to market, an amount equal to more than $50 million today. The canal was also used, as Washington had hoped, as a route to deliver pioneers into the western interior lands along the Ohio River and beyond.

House of Burgesses. When the British finally gave in and removed the hated act, Washington wrote to a friend that all "who were instrumental in procuring the repeal are entitled to the thanks of every British subject and have mine cordially."[20]

Washington did, on occasion, take a more active role in the protests. In late 1769, when the House of Burgesses wrote a document protesting a series of British taxes called the Townshend Duties, Washington was one of the first to sign. As events became more confrontational, Washington was not among the most active and fiery protestors. As late as 1774, with the Revolutionary War less than a year away, he still remained "a modest man, but sensible and speaks little—in action cool, like a Bishop at his prayers."[21]

But with each new act or step taken by the British government to hamper American trade, tax the citizens of the colonies, or place British troops in cities such as Boston, Philadelphia, and New York to keep protests at a minimum, Washington began to turn increasingly away from support of King George III and Parliament. By the 1770s, he began speaking against "our lordly Masters in Great Britain."[22] He even spoke to friends about the possibility of taking up arms against the British.

In the summer of 1774, Washington was selected as one of seven delegates from Virginia to attend a meeting of representatives from the 13 colonies, called the First Continental Congress. This gathering of more than 50 men was to discuss the ways in which the colonies might more effectively protest British actions.

In a letter to the brother of George William Fairfax, Washington's longtime friend, he put his political views on paper. To Bryan Fairfax, who favored a more peaceful response to British actions, Washington wrote:

As to your political sentiments, I would heartily join you in them . . . provided there was the most distant hope of success. But have we not tried this already? Have we not addressed the Lords? . . . And to what end? Does it not appear, as clear as the sun . . . that there is a regular, systematic plan formed to fix the right and practice of taxation upon us? . . . Do not all the debates . . . in the House of Commons . . . expressly declare that America must be taxed in aid of the British? . . . Ought we not to put our virtue and fortitude to the severest test?[23]

Test Your Knowledge

I As commander-in-chief of the Virginia militia, what was Washington's major challenge?

   a. Proving that the Virginia militia was better than the British Regulars.

   b. Protecting the capital of Virginia, Williamsburg, from attack.

   c. Protecting the 400-mile Virginia frontier.

   d. Providing protective cover for the British troops as they marched to Philadelphia.

2 In 1758, Washington was elected to serve in what legislative body?

   a. The British Parliament.

   b. The House of Representatives.

   c. The Virginia Senate.

   d. The Virginia House of Burgesses.

3 Who was Martha Dandridge Custis?

   a. George Washington's wife.

   b. George Washington's mother.

   c. The wealthy widow of Washington's half-brother.

   d. A woman who disguised herself as a man to fight in the French and Indian War.

4 What happened after the Treaty of Paris was signed?

    a. The French were forced to abandon all claims to Canada.

    b. The Ohio Country became British territory.

    c. Britain's national debt doubled.

    d. All of the above.

5 What event(s) contributed to Washington's changing attitude toward King George III and the British Parliament?

    a. The Stamp Act.

    b. The Townshend Duties.

    c. The stationing of British troops in Boston, New York, and Philadelphia.

    d. All of the above.

ANSWERS: 1. c; 2. d; 3. a; 4. d; 5. d

OUR RIGHTS AND OUR LIBERTIES

Commander-
in-Chief

Washington and his fellow delegates to the First
Continental Congress engaged in endless debates and
political discussions about how to protest British policy.
They came from all the colonies, and each man brought to
the meetings in Philadelphia his own view of the events that
had taken place over the previous decade. There was little

agreement between them on the direction they should take or the political stand they wanted to represent. After all, said John Adams, a delegate from Massachusetts, they were mostly strangers to one another, "not acquainted with each other's language, ideas, views, designs. They are, therefore, jealous of each other—fearful, timid, skittish."[24] Some wanted to make amends with King George. Others, such as Thomas Jefferson, spoke in favor of independence.

Washington was not comfortable with public speaking and remained quiet during the six weeks of meetings, preferring to listen and learn. He spent time after meetings socializing with his fellow delegates, especially in taverns. Before they adjourned their final session, the men of the First Continental Congress agreed to support a boycott of British goods and to meet again the following May as the Second Continental Congress.

Through the winter of 1774–1775, the situation between the Americans and British authorities deteriorated rapidly. The following spring, clashes between the colonists and the British led to war. When British troops marched near Boston in search of stores of patriot arms and gunpowder, as well as the patriot leaders Sam Adams and John Hancock, they clashed with militia troops gathered on the village green of Lexington. By the end of that April 1775 battle, eight young militiamen lay dead on the village common, and the shots fired early that morning launched the conflict that would become the American Revolutionary War. In writing to George William Fairfax, who had moved from Virginia to Britain with his wife, Sally, Washington sadly realized the full meaning of the Lexington fight: "Unhappy it is . . . to reflect . . . the once happy and peaceful plains of America are either to be drenched with Blood, or Inhabited by Slaves. Sad alternative! But can a virtuous Man hesitate in his choice?"[25]

Late the following month, the Second Continental Congress met in Philadelphia. Washington and his fellow delegates debated how to aid the militia troops in Massachusetts, where thousands of British troops were stationed. The delegates debated the creation of a Continental Army, one representing troops from every colony. While several men, some with greater wartime experience, were considered for the role of commander-in-chief of the Continental Army, John Adams placed Washington's name before his fellow delegates on

June 14. (Washington had shown his interest in the position by wearing his militia uniform to every meeting of the Congress.) The veteran of the French and Indian War was popular with his colleagues in the Congress. One delegate described the Virginia planter as "a fine figure and of a most easy and agreeable address."[26] The Virginia delegate was soon accepted unanimously. When chosen, Washington humbly recognized the scope of his new role, stating, "I do not think my self equal to the Command I am honoured with."[27] He also made it clear that he would not accept any pay for his service.

WASHINGTON TAKES COMMAND

With his appointment, George Washington, then 43 years old, was responsible for leading the Continental Army against a military considered to be the finest in the world. Within days of his appointment, he penned a letter to Martha, giving her the news. In that letter he wrote: "I hope that my undertaking . . . is designed to answer some good purpose."[28] On July 3, Washington arrived in Cambridge, outside Boston, to take command of the Continental Army. He found 15,000 anxious troops awaiting his arrival. The army that gathered

Delegates to the Second Continental Congress chose
Washington as commander-in-chief of the Continental
Army. He arrived in Cambridge, Massachusetts, in July
1775 to take command.

on the heights above Boston was hardly an army in any real sense. Instead, it "consisted of farmers, plowboys, backwoodsmen, counting house clerks, stevedores, all of whom were fighting a personal war."[29]

The new commander-in-chief understood the problems he faced. His troops were not a trained, regular force. His army was green and unreliable. They were not disciplined, a fact that was as galling to Washington as it was to the British. They were truly "minutemen." They came from parts unknown, in a minute, and in another minute had disappeared. One historian noted, "They were always present when provisions were distributed but disappeared when it was time for drill. Their lack of organization, discipline . . . [begs] description. Each body of troops, being from a different colony, considered itself independent . . . Furthermore they were there only on extremely short-term enlistments. This was the human material Washington had at his disposal . . . He fared even worse on money and supplies: lack of funds, no authority to raise any, a shortage of uniforms, stores, equipment, powder, ammunition."[30]

Although Washington created a better prepared and disciplined army over the next few years, lack of supplies remained a problem through the entire eight years of war. Washington spent months instilling discipline in his men. He ordered them to build fortifications and improve sanitation in the camps. He worked to improve their morale. No battles were fought that summer or fall; Washington did not have adequate artillery to drive the British out of Boston. When chilly winds began to blow, signaling the arrival of autumn, the Virginia general began ordering his men to build barracks. The fight for Boston would have to wait until spring.

That winter did witness action on the revolutionary battlefield. American troops under the command of Colonel Benedict Arnold marched north up the St. Lawrence River Valley and attacked the British garrison at Quebec, Canada, an attack that would fail. Arnold also participated in an attack with volunteers called the Green Mountain Boys, under the command of a Vermonter named Ethan Allen, capturing the British garrison at Fort Ticonderoga in upstate New York.

The fort had something Washington needed desperately—siege cannon. When he received word of Ticonderoga's capture, he ordered the cannon brought to Boston, stating that "no Trouble or Expence [sic] must be spared to obtain them."[31] Through the snow and across ice-frozen rivers, Ethan Allen and his men dragged

43 cannon and 16 mortars back to Boston, hauling the heavy artillery on ox-drawn sleds, reaching Washington in February 1776. By March 4, Washington had overseen the fortification of the heights above the city with this siege artillery. The following morning, the British troops in Boston were stunned by the presence of cannon in Cambridge Heights.

Within two weeks, General Howe and his forces evacuated the city. The victory, in which no shots were fired, went to Washington. Pleased with the turn of events, Washington wrote to the President of the Continental Congress, John Hancock: "It is with the greatest pleasure I inform you that on Sunday last . . . the Ministerial Army evacuated the Town of Boston, and that the Forces of the United Colonies are now in actual Possession thereof."[32]

THE YEAR OF INDEPENDENCE

The spring of 1776 brought other changes in the American effort to liberate the colonies from British control. The cause of independence was gaining ground. In late 1775, a minority of Americans favored independence. But during the early months of the following year, public sentiment began to change, led in part by the publication of a pamphlet titled *Common Sense*. It was the work of a recent English immigrant to America, Thomas Paine. He put into words the feelings of a growing number of Americans: "Every thing that is right or reasonable pleads for separation. The blood of the slain, the weeping voice of nature cries, 'TIS TIME TO PART.' Even the distance at which the Almighty hath placed England and America is a strong and natural proof, that the authority of the one over the other, was never the design of Heaven."[33]

Words such as these gave Americans a new sense of purpose in their opposition to British authority and power. Other events had the same effect. While Arnold's campaign against Quebec had failed, another American assault, this one against Montreal, had succeeded. The British had been removed from Boston and, by April 4, Washington had set out with his army toward New York to take up defensive positions. A British attempt to capture Charleston, South Carolina, through a naval expedition, had also failed. Through the remainder of the spring and even as late as midsummer, the Americans seemed to have the British at bay. From April through June, "there was no British regular force within the thirteen colonies, except for one . . . pushing down from Canada into northern New York."[34] Optimism marked the patriot movement, causing Congress to seriously consider the possibility of declaring America's independence.

By May 1776, the majority of Americans had rejected the idea of reconciliation with Great Britain. The king was looked on as a villain, one who so disregarded the colonies that he had hired German mercenaries—Hessians—whom he paid to fight against the Americans. By July 2, the Congress had voted in favor of independence from Britain and, two days later, voted to adopt a "Declaration of Independence."

Washington received official word of the declaration on July 9 at his headquarters in New York. He announced it that day in his General Orders to his officers and men, and ordered brigades to be formed that evening, "where the declaration of Congress . . . is to be read with an audible voice."[35] Washington had hopes that "this important Event will serve as a fresh incentive to every officer, and soldier, to act with Fidelity and Courage, as knowing that now the peace and safety of his Country depends (under God) solely on the success of our arms."[36]

In July 1776, Congress voted in favor of independence from Britain. Washington received the news on July 9, and ordered the Declaration of Independence to be read aloud to his men.

Washington's words could not have been truer. A week earlier, a British fleet of more than 100 ships with 10,000 men on board had dropped anchor in New York Harbor. The battle for New York City was about to begin.

Test Your Knowledge

I What agreement was reached by the First Continental Congress?

   a. To declare independence from British rule.

   b. To support a boycott of British goods.

   c. To send troops to Boston.

   d. To appoint George Washington as commander-in-chief of the Continental Army.

2 Where were the first shots in the conflict that became the Revolutionary War fired?

   a. In Philadelphia, Pennsylvania.

   b. In Yorktown, Virginia.

   c. In Lexington, Massachusetts.

   d. In Trenton, New Jersey.

3 How did Washington demonstrate his interest in being appointed commander-in-chief of the Continental Army?

   a. He wore his uniform to meetings of the Second Continental Congress.

   b. He discussed possible battle strategies with his fellow delegates.

   c. He distributed copies of a report detailing the strengths and weaknesses of the British Army.

   d. He was an outspoken critic of the other candidates for the position.

4 When Washington arrived in Cambridge to assume command of the Continental Army, what phrase most accurately describes the army he was to lead into battle?

   a. Highly trained marksmen skilled in battle.

   b. Unified troops who described themselves as Americans.

   c. Well-equipped colonial militia who welcomed their new commander-in-chief.

   d. An undisciplined, unreliable collection of men with little experience in combat.

5 When Washington learned of the formal declaration of independence, what was his response?

   a. He nodded briefly, then returned to forming plans for the next battle.

   b. He was concerned that the announcement might prove a distraction to his troops.

   c. He ordered that the declaration be read aloud to his men.

   d. He distributed copies to all of his men.

ANSWERS: 1. b; 2. c; 3. a; 4. d; 5. c

OUR RIGHTS AND OUR LIBERTIES

Victory at Yorktown

For the patriots, the highlight of 1776 was the move by Congress calling for independence. Yet the six months that followed to year's end were difficult days for the American cause, especially for General Washington. By August, the British had landed thousands of troops and Washington was vastly outnumbered. Many of his troops were unreliable, and only serving enlistments for two or three months. With them, Washington had to defend a front stretching for 15 miles.

On August 31, after the British commander General William Howe began placing 30,000 men ashore, he found the American left flank unprotected, and the battle of Long Island erupted. Howe nearly captured Washington's entire army. A night evacuation by Washington across the fog-covered East River allowed his men to escape to Manhattan. Some of those troops who evacuated across the river were informed personally of the approaching British by Washington, who rode hard on horseback to Fort Lee. The garrison there quickly abandoned their encampment in the middle of preparing a meal, leaving their cooking pots behind.

For weeks, Washington dodged the superior numbers of the British until he was able to retreat to New Jersey. However, he lost 3,000 of his men when they were captured at Fort Washington, on the north end of Manhattan. During these weeks, General Washington came close to losing the war. For months, he had been predicting, "We expect a very bloody summer of it at New York."[37] By September 1776, his prediction had come true.

With New York City lost, Washington and his men had been soundly beaten and their morale began to decline. Over the following months, the British pursued Washington's forces until the Redcoats drove them out of New York State in mid-November. By then, Washington's army was falling apart, as many of his troops decided to go home after their enlistments ran out. Some did not even wait, but chose to abandon the cause. By year's end, Washington was desperate. His army had dwindled to only 3,500 men. Many were prepared to leave the army when their enlistments expired at the end of the year. Discouraged, the Virginia general wrote to a cousin on December 10: "Our only dependence now is upon the speedy enlistment of a new army. If this fails, I think the game will be pretty well up."[38]

MIRACLE ON THE DELAWARE

In the face of an uncertain future for the patriot cause, Washington delivered a victory on Christmas Eve. With his men encamped in Pennsylvania (where they had been chased by pursuing British troops that fall), the American general planned to attack a Hessian garrison of 1,500 men across the Delaware River at Trenton,

New Jersey. He knew the German mercenaries would drink heavily in celebration of the Christmas holiday and that he might be able to surprise them by crossing the icy waters of the Delaware under cover of darkness. It was a plan based on long odds. But Washington needed a miracle.

Washington's crossing of the Delaware that Christmas Eve has become the stuff of legend. The night temperatures were frigid, and British patrols were everywhere. Simply getting his men across the river undetected was considered, by some of his fellow officers, to be impossible. Yet on Christmas morning, the Germans at Trenton were surprised by the Americans, who attacked with fixed bayonets since an overnight sleet storm had dampened their gunpowder. The American victory at Trenton provided Washington with the win he needed. Days later, he experienced another victory at Princeton, where he routed a British force. When Washington's men went into permanent winter quarters at Morristown, New Jersey, it was with the Continental Army still intact.

Washington pulled off these victories when his army was on the edge of collapse. Trenton and Princeton were actually small battles. Although Washington

Washington's surprise attack on Hessian soldiers at Trenton provided the Americans with a victory just as the Continental Army was on the verge of collapse.

ended 1776 and opened 1777 with two victories, he would not win a single battle for more than four years. Having already lost several battles over New York City, in 1777 he added to his losses. In September, he was defeated at Brandywine Creek in Pennsylvania, followed by an October loss at nearby Germantown.

Why, then, given such losses on the battlefield, is George Washington remembered as such a great leader during the American Revolutionary War? Because, despite such failures to defeat an enemy who normally came to the battlefield better trained, better equipped, better armed, better clothed, and better fed than their American opponents, Washington managed to keep his army in the field. Even when his men faced extreme hardships, many remained loyal to their commander-in-chief. Washington's true ability to lead had more to do with keeping his army together, rather than bringing about victories in combat.

MORE YEARS OF WAR

There were low points for both Washington and his army during the war. Perhaps the most difficult months of the war were those spent during the winter of 1777–1778 at Valley Forge, Pennsylvania. After a difficult year of fighting and avoiding capture at the hands of the British, Washington's men limped into their winter encampment on December 19, 1777, in the middle of a freezing sleet storm. Many of the men were without shoes, and had to wrap rags around their feet. Washington wrote, "You might have tracked the army . . . to Valley Forge by the blood of their feet."[39] Hurriedly, the men began building log huts for shelter. These shelters were not finished until mid-January. In the meantime, the difficulties of that December—a lack of food, outbreaks of disease, poor sanitation, a lack of blankets and adequate clothing—reduced Washington's forces dramatically. Eleven thousand men arrived at Valley Forge that month. By New Year's Day, they only numbered 6,000. Five thousand had either deserted or died.

Through those terrible winter months, Washington heard the constant cries, complaints, and criticism from his men. In a letter to Congress, he observed his own personal agony concerning the poor circumstances his men were enduring: "I feel superabundantly for them, and, from my soul, I pity those miseries, which it is neither in my power to relieve or prevent."[40] In addition, Washington faced a challenge to his leadership that winter. Several congressmen and some of Washington's own generals, including General Gates, plotted to remove the Virginia leader from his position as commander-in-chief. (Gates was riding high after having defeated a British army in New York in October at the battle of Saratoga.) A year earlier, Thomas Paine had penned another pamphlet, *The Crisis*, in which he wrote: "These are the times that try men's souls."[41] For Washington, that time had arrived once again. But through such difficult times, Washington did not give up hope.

By March, events again turned in his favor. The plot to remove him had fallen apart and failed. His army emerged from their wintry ordeal ready to fight again and new recruits began arriving with the spring. By May, Washington received wonderful news. The French announced that they were ready to begin helping the Americans in their struggle against Britain. (Ironically, it was the victory of General Gates at Saratoga the previous October that had convinced the French that the Americans might be capable of winning their revolution after all.) They were also "impressed by Washington's successes as well as by the manner of his defeats."[42]

THE BATTLE OF MONMOUTH

The following month, Washington saw an opportunity to take up the battle against the British once again. Much of the British army had spent the winter in Philadelphia, and their new commander, General Henry Clinton, decided to move them to New York, since the capture of Philadelphia had not resulted in the collapse of the rebel American government. (Congress had

The winter encampment at Valley Forge, Pennsylvania, brought great hardship to Washington's troops, reducing his force by nearly half. Here, Washington is shown praying before leading his army out of Valley Forge to attack British troops marching from Philadelphia to New York.

relocated to Baltimore.) As the British began to move, Washington ordered his men out of Valley Forge, intent on attacking the enemy column. Some of his officers thought the idea madness. They were certain that the American army could not weather an open battle against British Regulars. But Washington would not listen. His men finally caught up with Clinton's army near Monmouth Courthouse, New Jersey. Here they attacked the rear of the British advance.

On an extremely hot day—June 28—Washington launched his attack. But the general whom Washington ordered to lead the assault, Charles Lee, was unconvinced he could succeed and turned and retreated too quickly. Furious, Washington rode forward, reorganized his men and for the remainder of the day, the battle of Monmouth Courthouse unfolded. The Americans stood their ground admirably. Although the fight never developed into a full-scale engagement, it reminded everyone of Washington's ability to rally his men and display an aggressive spirit even when victory was uncertain. The fight boosted the spirits of his army as nothing had since Trenton. It would be the last important battle for Washington's army for the next three years.

Clinton's forces did reach New York, and Washington flanked his army and took position up the Hudson River at West Point to keep a close eye on Clinton's future movements. But Clinton made none. A cautious general, he remained in New York, having no desire to risk his army in a fight with the Continental Army. Instead, the British commander shifted the war to the southern states for the next two years, capturing Savannah by December and Charleston in August 1780.

ONE LAST BATTLE

Washington spent those two years trying to hold his army together. But his biggest problem was not the British army. Instead, it was the lack of supplies his men received from Congress. During the winters of 1778–1779 and 1779–1780, he had to deal with several mutinies led by small groups of his own men. Such mutinies were usually caused by a lack of food and pay. On Christmas Eve, 1779, Washington was forced to order corn intended for horses to be ground into meal for his men. When Martha visited her husband in camp during the summer of 1780, she found him uncertain and depressed: "The pore General [was] so unhappy that it distressed me exceedingly."[43] Even as late as April 1781, Washington was still struggling to get supplies for his troops, writing in a letter to Congress, "We are at the end of our tether."[44]

Victory did finally come for Washington and his loyal troops during the fall of 1781. British troops under

A Surrender of Errors

The surrender of the British at Yorktown signaled the end of the war. For Washington it was a great victory. During the official surrender ceremonies, it was the custom for the defeated general to hand his sword to the commander of the winning side. On the day of the official surrender, the two sides gathered their troops together opposite one another. As Washington waited on horseback for Cornwallis, a British brigadier general approached in his place. When he reached Washington, the subordinate officer tried to hand his sword to the French commander at his side, General Rochambeau. Rochambeau refused the sword, telling the British officer, "You are mistaken. The Commander in Chief of our army is on the right," as he pointed to Washington.*

The brigadier general then turned to Washington, introducing himself as Brigadier Charles O'Hara. He the command of General Lord Cornwallis had menaced the southern states for three years, winning such engagements as the battle of Camden in South Carolina in August 1780. But rebel forces had continued to harass Cornwallis's army until he was forced to retreat north to Virginia. By September, the British general was

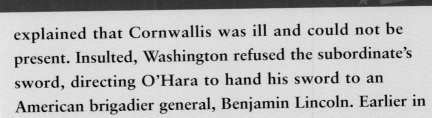

explained that Cornwallis was ill and could not be present. Insulted, Washington refused the subordinate's sword, directing O'Hara to hand his sword to an American brigadier general, Benjamin Lincoln. Earlier in the war, Lincoln had lost the battle of Charleston at the hands of a British general, who had disgraced Lincoln by not allowing the American commander's men to carry their flags at the surrender ceremony. For Lincoln, accepting a British sword was sweet revenge.

Although Cornwallis shirked his duty that day, Washington's victory was complete. In defeating the British general, the Continental Army took more than 8,000 British troops prisoner, captured nearly 250 cannon and thousands of muskets.

* Richard M. Ketchum, *The World of George Washington* (New York: American Heritage Publishing, 1974), 174.

bottled up in the little tobacco port of Yorktown waiting for transport by ship out of harm's way. But a French fleet blocked the British navy's access to Chesapeake Bay, leaving Cornwallis stranded.

Hurriedly, Washington moved his men south toward Yorktown. During this march, Washington's forces swelled in number as new recruits, anxious to end the long revolutionary conflict, joined him. By the time he reached Williamsburg, near Yorktown, the number of French and American troops present was nearly 10,000. Soon, that number swelled to 16,000. At hand was the final battle of the war. On September 28, the siege of Yorktown began. Over the next two weeks, Cornwallis was further hemmed as Continental troops captured British positions in and around Yorktown. Finally, on October 19, 1781, Cornwallis surrendered, handing Washington his greatest victory, along with 8,000 British Regulars as prisoners. For the first time since the war had begun on an April day in 1775 at Lexington and Concord, the end of the American Revolutionary War seemed near.

Test Your Knowledge

I Why was the victory at Trenton so important to Washington?

   a. Morale had declined following the loss of New York City.

   b. Many of Washington's troops were planning to leave when their enlistments expired at the end of the year.

   c. It was one of the few battles Washington won during the Revolutionary War.

   d. All of the above.

2 Why was the encampment at Valley Forge so difficult?

   a. British forces attacked several times from their camp in Philadelphia.

   b. The men were sick and lacked adequate food and clothing.

   c. The hot weather caused an outbreak of disease and made long marches difficult.

   d. Washington was temporarily relieved of his command by a dissatisfied Congress.

3 What was General Charles Lee's role in the Battle of Monmouth?

   a. He commanded the British Army marching to New York.

   b. He drafted the plan to attack the British from the rear as they marched north.

   c. Ordered to lead the assault, he turned and ordered a retreat when he thought the plan could not succeed.

   d. He assisted Washington in rallying the troops and leading them to victory.

4 What was one of Washington's greatest challenges in leading the Continental Army?

   a. A lack of adequate food and pay for his men.

   b. His lack of formal education.

   c. His age.

   d. His army's fear of the superior training and supplies of the British forces.

5 What happened as Washington led his men south to Yorktown?

   a. Many soldiers deserted.

   b. Many new recruits joined him.

   c. Congress ordered him back to protect Philadelphia.

   d. General Cornwallis quickly ordered an attack and Washington's troops were defeated.

ANSWERS: 1. d; 2. b; 3. c; 4. a; 5. b

8

America's First President

Although the battle of Yorktown marked the end of major fighting between the Continental Army and the British, another two years passed before a treaty of peace was signed in Paris between the two warring powers. (Two of the American negotiators were Benjamin Franklin and John Adams.) During those years, Washington kept his army in the field, encamped near West Point, New York. Once the peace treaty was signed on September 3, 1783, it was only a matter of months before the British troops left America. By early December, Washington met with his officers at New York's Fraunces Tavern and gave his good-byes, tears streaming down the faces of everyone in the room, including their commander. The general then left to report to Congress in Annapolis, Maryland. It had been nearly nine years since Washington had left his home to lead the Continental Army through the revolution. When he reached Mount Vernon, on Christmas Eve, Martha was waiting for him, and, in every window of the house, a candle shone brightly.

Once again, Washington intended to retire to private life at his beloved home along the Potomac River. He wanted to fill his days with the details of farm and family. But it soon became clear that the new government that had been created in place of British rule was not perfect. In fact, it was seriously flawed. In 1781, Congress had adopted a form of constitutional government based on a document called the Articles of Confederation. Under this system, the newly created states held power superior to that of the national government, which consisted almost entirely of a one-house legislature. There was no chief executive, no national court system, and no system of taxation. This weak confederacy government had no power to engage in war, make treaties with foreign nations, or even coin money without the consent of the states. In only a few short years, the independent-minded states were quarreling with one another, and the system was on the verge of collapse.

By 1786, many Americans were disappointed in their new government. Washington was one of them. Early that year, in a conversation with friends, the retired general noted, "Something must be done, or the fabric must fall, for it is certainly tottering."[45]

In January, the Virginia legislature invited delegates from every state to attend a convention in Annapolis, Maryland, to discuss their mutual problems concerning interstate trade. Five states attended. Before they finished business, one of the Virginia delegates, James Madison, called for a convention to be held in Philadelphia the following year to change the structure of the Articles of Confederation and improve the national government. Washington was chosen as a delegate from Virginia. At the convention, the 55-year-old Virginia planter,

In 1787, Washington was chosen as the president of the
Constitutional Convention, which created a new form of
government for the United States.

racked by rheumatism, was chosen as the president of
the Constitutional Convention.

A NEW CONSTITUTION

The convention did not fulfill its goal of rewriting the
Articles of Confederation that summer. Instead, the
convention realized the weaknesses of the existing government and decided to scrap the original constitution.

In its place, they created a new form of government, one in which power was embodied in the people. A two-house legislature was established, including a House of Representatives and a Senate. The new constitution established a national court system and an executive branch to enforce the laws passed by Congress. The head of that branch was the Chief Executive. Electors were selected to choose someone to fill that important and new role of government. Few Americans were as well known as George Washington. Although he did not campaign or seek the office, the electors chose him unanimously. John Adams was chosen as the nation's first vice president.

On April 30, 1789, Washington arrived in the new American capital at New York City, which remained the seat of government until the following year, when it was moved to Philadelphia. Washington took the oath of office at a site along Wall Street, as a great crowd cheered warmly for their new president. Earlier in April, from his home at Mount Vernon, he wrote to his old friend, Henry Knox, "I am sensible, that I am embarking the voice of my Countrymen and a good name of my own, on this voyage, but what returns will be made for them—Heaven alone can foretell."[46]

WASHINGTON'S INAUGURATION AS PRESIDENT.

Washington was inaugurated as president in 1789 in New York, which would serve as the first capital briefly, before the federal government was moved to Philadelphia.

PRESIDENT WASHINGTON

With every step Washington took as president, he defined the office. "Few . . . can realize the difficult and delicate part which a man in my situation had to act . . . I walk on untrodden ground."[47] Washington was careful as he established the role of the president, knowing that he would be setting a standard for others to follow.

Even the question of what the new president should be called was a subject for consideration. John Adams favored the lofty title "His Highness, the President of the United States of America and Protector of their Liberties." Washington, however, decided that the title "Mr. President" would be enough.

Another important question for Washington was how much he should make himself available to the people. He rode around the streets of New York on a white horse, sitting on a leopard-skin saddlecloth. He rented some of the best houses in both New York and Philadelphia, refusing an offer to live in the mansion of New York's governor, George Clinton. He would not accept any private invitations to dinner, wanting to avoid any hint at favoritism. The new president did attend the theater often, for he loved plays, and there managed to relax among friends and acquaintances. He established a ritual reception every Tuesday afternoon while living in New York (Martha moved them to Fridays when they lived in Philadelphia), which was open to the public, but only to men. (Those who came to meet and greet the president had to dress appropriately, however.) At these receptions, Washington wore a velvet jacket, yellow gloves, and a powdered wig. He held a military-style cockade hat and wore a gleaming sword at his side.

To help him in his important decisions, Washington selected his chief advisors, men who would serve in his cabinet. He selected Thomas Jefferson as his Secretary of State, Alexander Hamilton as Secretary of the Treasury, Henry Knox as Secretary of War, and Edmund Randolph as Attorney General. These men served the president well and loyally, even if Jefferson and Hamilton did not like each other. By the fall of 1790, Washington had appointed nearly 125 men to government jobs, including Supreme Court appointments.

During Washington's first full year as president, while facing the difficulties of the office, he experienced a tremendous personal loss. For some time, his mother, Mary Ball Washington, had been suffering with breast cancer. Although widowed at an early age, Mrs. Washington had never remarried and continued to rely heavily on her famous son for her care and comfort. Washington and his mother were never extremely close (she was a constant complainer, even as Washington stepped into the role of president). But when she died, during the summer of 1789, Washington mourned her passing with great sorrow.

PROBLEMS AT HOME AND ABROAD

As a new nation, under a new form of government, the United States experienced many challenges during Washington's presidency. One of the greatest was caused by a lack of money. Yet Washington's Secretary of the Treasury, Alexander Hamilton, worked tirelessly to put the young nation on a sound economic footing. He encouraged payment of the government's debts in full. He called for the assumption of millions of dollars in state debts. Hamilton encouraged the development of American trade and manufacturing, and called for the establishment of a national bank and a national mint.

What Were We Like as a Nation in 1790?

The beginning of Washington's presidency marked the end of many years of protest, rebellion, and war. The people of the new United States looked forward to a new era of nationalism. But what did it mean to be a new *American*? What were we like as a nation, as a people, in 1790?

To begin, a census was taken that year, the first national headcount. It revealed a nation consisting of 3,929,214 people. They were generally equally divided between the northern states and the southern states. The vast majority of Americans were white. More than 50 percent were of English ancestry; 20 percent were Scottish or Irish. Another 20 percent were black. There were significant populations of Germans, French, Swedish, Dutch, and Finns, who had also made America their home.

Nearly all of the four million people counted in the 1790 census were living in rural areas, on farms and plantation estates. Only about 200,000 people lived in the two dozen or so larger towns or cities in the United States, those with at least 2,500 inhabitants or more. The largest were Boston, Philadelphia, New York, Baltimore, and Charleston. Only two—New York and Philadelphia—had a population of more than 25,000 residents.

Most of these Americans lived in approximately the same areas and regions people had lived in for nearly two centuries—along the eastern Atlantic seaboard. A relatively small number of Americans were living west of the Appalachians in 1790. But the West was the fastest growing region in the country. During the 1790s, Kentucky and Tennessee tripled in population. Kentucky, in 1800, could boast a population greater than five of the original 13 states.

During the decade after 1790, the new United States made great strides in its national growth, development, and progress. In 1790, there were only three banks nationwide, and they held assets totaling less than $5 million, about one dollar per person living in the entire country. Between 1790 and 1800, hundreds of banks, corporations, and other financial institutions were established. The number of newspapers doubled. Seventy-five post offices in 1790 became almost 1,000 by 1800. Exports more than tripled from $29 million to $107 million. Eleven factories and mechanized mills were constructed, producing everything from glass to textiles to nails to guns. From the end of the American Revolutionary War to 1800, 17 new colleges were chartered, including new medical schools.

George Washington presided over a rapidly developing United States and helped support its early expansion. The president addressed this growth and prosperity in a speech to Congress in 1795, as he invited Congressmen to "join with me, in profound gratitude to the Author of all good, for the numerous, and extraordinary blessings we enjoy."*

* George Washington, *Writings* (New York: The Library of America, 1991), 919.

He also called for a tax on the production and sale of such goods as carriages, snuff, and—under great controversy—whiskey.

The new president faced many serious problems. Within a few weeks of Washington's first inauguration, revolution broke out in France. As the rebellion to establish a republican form of government expanded, the French king was removed from power. Other European monarchies then declared war on France to restore the dethroned monarchy. Facing the military power of such countries as England, Spain, Austria, and Prussia, the French revolutionary government appealed to the United States for help. Both countries had signed a treaty of friendship and alliance in 1778, which had brought the French into the American Revolutionary War as an ally. Now, to the French, it was America's turn to help them.

These circumstances put Washington in a difficult position. The people of the United States were extremely divided in their support for either the British or the French. Even in Washington's own cabinet, Jefferson favored helping the French while Hamilton sided with the British. But Washington took no sides. In April 1793, just days after taking office in his second term as president, Washington wisely issued a proclamation of neutrality, declaring the country's need for "conduct friendly and impartial towards [all the European nations at war]."[48] For his decision, Washington was highly criticized.

In 1792, as the end of his first term approached, Washington was certain he would soon retire, once again, to his home at Mount Vernon. However, many Americans hoped that he would serve a second term. Jefferson, Hamilton, Knox, and Virginia congressman James Madison worked hard to persuade Washington to serve four more years. Jefferson wrote to Washington, "Your being at the helm will be more than an answer to every argument which can be used to alarm and lead the people . . . into violence or secession. North and South will hang together if they have you to hang on."[49]

Test Your Knowledge

I What were the weaknesses of the Articles of Confederation?

   a. The individual states held more power than the national government.

   b. There was no chief executive and no system of taxation.

   c. The states could not reach agreement on the coining of money, the signing of treaties, or other matters of national interest.

   d. All of the above.

2 Which city first served as the nation's capital?

   a. Philadelphia.

   b. Williamsburg.

   c. New York.

   d. Washington, D.C.

3 Who served as the nation's first vice president?

   a. Thomas Jefferson.

   b. John Adams.

   c. Alexander Hamilton.

   d. John Hancock.

4 What policies helped bring an end to the financial challenges facing the new United States of America?

   a. All government debts had to be paid in full.

   b. A national bank and a national mint were established.

   c. Taxes were placed on carriages, snuff, and whiskey.

   d. All of the above.

5 What position did Washington take in the conflict between the British and French following the French revolution?

   a. He stated that the United States would remain neutral.

   b. He supported the French revolutionary government, believing that its ideals were similar to those that had inspired the American Revolution.

   c. He formed an alliance with Britain, hoping to increase trade and ease the country's economic struggles.

   d. He attempted to form an alliance with Britain, but was snubbed by the British Parliament.

ANSWERS: 1. d; 2. c; 3. b; 4. d; 5. a

A Final
Farewell

Washington did agree to a second term and was reelected, again unanimously, by the electoral college. Adams was reelected as vice president. Washington was 61 years old when he was inaugurated on March 4, 1793. His second term in office soon proved even more challenging than his first had been.

Washington had to deal with several important foreign problems and issues during his second term as president. The British still occupied forts on American soil in the Northwest Territory. They had agreed to evacuate such military posts under the Treaty of 1783, but were dragging their feet to embarrass the young, relatively weak United States government. To complicate matters, the British were arming Northwestern Indians, such as the powerful Shawnee, against the westward-moving Americans. In response, Washington sent a diplomat, John Jay, to London to negotiate a treaty. Although he had little to offer the British, he was able to arrange an agreement, known as Jay's Treaty. The British agreed to leave the Northwest, but did not completely abandon the last of their forts there until 1796.

Meanwhile, elsewhere along the frontier, violence against Hamilton's new whiskey tax was causing trouble, particularly in the backwoods of Pennsylvania. This tax, once implemented, sparked anger among the frontiersmen who privately produced whiskey and other forms of alcohol. In 1794, when farmers and distillers in four western Pennsylvania counties refused to pay the tax, armed themselves, and attacked federal officials, Washington was forced to respond. The so-called

"Whiskey Rebellion" caused the President to call up 15,000 troops, including more than 12,000 militiamen. Washington, as commander-in-chief, decided to lead the army himself. He had not worn a uniform as a military commander in more than a decade. But the rebellion, in the face of this dramatic show of government force, fizzled out and its supporters scattered. Similar protests against the British had been common in the years leading up to the American Revolutionary War. But Washington made it clear that he did not intend to tolerate riots and violent mob demonstrations.

By the end of his second term, Washington could look back on a presidency of successes and failures, including unresolved frustrations. Jay's Treaty had sparked great criticism. However, in 1795, Washington returned to popularity through another foreign treaty, this one with Spain. An American diplomat and nego-tiator, Thomas Pinckney of South Carolina, negotiated a treaty that gave Americans the right to ship their goods from their frontier homes down to the port of New Orleans at the mouth of the Mississippi River and ship them out as exports without paying a duty. The treaty was highly popular with western settlers, who needed a ready market for their farm products.

Another successful treaty came in Washington's last full year in office. After the U.S. Army successfully defeated several allied Northwestern tribes, Native American leaders accepted an agreement that forced them to cede much of the lands they claimed in Ohio. This treaty helped make the Trans-Appalachian West safer for Americans heading west.

This was critical, as the western frontier was expanding. By the end of his second term, Washington had witnessed the addition of three new states: Vermont, Kentucky, and Tennessee. Growth and progress were everywhere. New turnpike roads were being built, as well as much-needed canal projects to help develop American transportation. The new capital, Federal City (today known as Washington, D.C.), was being laid out on the Maryland side of the Potomac, only a few miles upriver from Mount Vernon.

As Washington's second term drew to a close, many of his supporters suggested that he serve a third term as president. But Washington had had enough of public life. Political parties had developed during his presidency, formed by followers of Hamilton and Jefferson. Strong opposition to some of his decisions had weighed heavily on him. He chose not to run for a third term, letting the public know in a farewell address issued on September 19, 1796. In this final message to the American people, Washington stated his goal as president: "With me, a predominant motive has been, to endeavour to gain time for our country to settle and mature its yet recent institutions, and to progress without interruption, to that degree of strength and consistency, which is necessary to give it, humanly speaking, the command of its own fortunes."[50]

As a delegate, a representative, a general, a commander-in-chief, and as president, Washington had served his country long and hard. He wanted to return to his home and family on his Virginia plantation.

BACK HOME AT MOUNT VERNON

That fall, John Adams was elected as America's second president, while Thomas Jefferson was chosen as his vice president. At Adams's Inauguration, Washington was present. Adams later wrote: "In the chamber of the House of Representatives was a multitude as great as the space would contain, and I believe scarcely a dry eye but Washington's."[51] Washington shed no tears. In his diary that day, he did not even mention the Inauguration: "Much such a day as yesterday in all

Washington spent his final years at Mount Vernon with Martha and his grandchildren.

respects. Mercury [today's temperature] at 41."[52] He was ready to retire. He was ready for the quiet and peacefulness he knew awaited him at Mount Vernon. Washington soon set out from Philadelphia for Mount Vernon. Along his route home, he was greeted by crowds in every small town and village.

Life back at Mount Vernon proved rewarding to the retired George Washington. His two youngest grandchildren—Eleanor Parke Custis and George Washington Custis—lived at Mount Vernon, their parents having died prematurely. (Their father, John Parke Custis, had died of a fever during the siege at Yorktown in 1781, at the age of 27.) Washington's home was always filled with guests and visiting relatives. Family members sometimes came for a visit and stayed for months, or even years. But Washington turned no one away.

Washington had returned to life as a country gentleman, one who owned a Virginia plantation where slaves worked in the fields and the outbuildings. The former president's lands had grown over the years. At his retirement, they fronted the Potomac River for ten miles and in from the river an average of four or five miles. Although he had some trouble adjusting to private life, he found a routine for himself, which he summed up in a letter written two months after his return to Mount Vernon:

I begin my [day] with the Sun . . . I examine the state of things [at Mount Vernon] . . . by that time I have accomplished these matters, breakfast a little after seven o'clock . . . is ready. This over, I mount my horse and ride round my farms, which employs me until it is time to dress for dinner; at which I rarely miss seeing strange faces; come, as they say, out of respect to me. . . . The usual time of sitting at Table; a walk, and Tea, bring me within the dawn of Candlelight. . . . I resolve, that, as soon as the glimmering taper, supplies the place of the great luminary, I will retire to my writing Table and acknowledge the letters I have received; but when the lights are brought, I feel tired.[53]

When guests were in the house, George and Martha entertained in the evenings. But on most nights, Washington was in bed by nine o'clock.

In his retirement, Washington did find satisfaction and rest. However, he was sometimes bored and lonely. In 1798, when he was approached to return to a public life of sorts, he hesitated. That year, war between the United States and France over seizures of American ships on the high seas seemed on the horizon. President Adams called Washington out of retirement to take command of the army. Reluctantly, he agreed, but the crisis with France passed, and Washington stayed home.

Washington and Slavery

The story of George Washington frequently focuses on his role in the Revolutionary War or as the first to hold the office of president of the United States. He is remembered as a surveyor, frontier explorer, militia commander, planter, and patriot. However, Washington was something else as well—a slave owner.

It is difficult for modern readers to understand how a man like Washington could fight for independence and liberty and still own slaves. Today, some consider Washington's practice of slaveholding as a reason to reduce his importance as a Founding Father. To understand Washington's actions, it is important to understand what role slavery had in the world of George Washington.

For more than 250 years, slavery was practiced in America. As early as the days of the first permanent English colony in North America—Jamestown—blacks were landed by ship along the Atlantic Coast, delivered from Africa, and put to work as either servants or slaves. By the time of Washington's birth, slavery was an established system that provided black labor in all of the 13 colonies. No colony had more slaves by 1750 than Virginia. As a young man, Washington accepted the existence of black slaves without much thought.

However, as he grew older, Washington began to understand how slavery could destroy lives and families. Even before the Revolutionary War, he decided that he

would "not sell or move any slave without that slave's consent."* Washington did not want to break up families and began speaking of slavery as a "misfortune."**

By the time of the American Revolution, he was having more serious doubts about slavery. As commander-in-chief, he began offering freedom to any slave who enlisted in the Continental Army. After the Revolution, he wrote to an English admirer "that nothing but the rooting out of slavery can perpetuate the existence of our union by consolidating it in a common bond of principle."***

Washington continued to rely on slave labor on his farms. He was, compared to other owners, kind to his black workers. By 1788, all five of his farm overseers were black, and he was recognizing slave marriages among his slaves. At the end of his presidency, he left several slave house servants behind in Pennsylvania, knowing that they would be freed automatically under state law if they did not return to Virginia.

Despite these comments and small gestures, Washington died a slave owner. He did take, however, a drastic step at his death. In his will, Washington stated that all of his slaves should be given their freedom.

---

* James Thomas Flexner, *George Washington: Anguish and Farewell (1793–1799)* (Boston: Little, Brown and Company, 1969), 386.

** Ibid, 387.

*** James Thomas Flexner, *Washington: The Indispensable Man* (Boston: Little, Brown and Company, 1974), 386.

WASHINGTON'S FINAL DAYS

The next year would be the last for George Washington. On December 12, 1799, he returned from his usual journey around his property, having become chilled. While out on his horse, snow had begun to fall, the temperature plummeted, and there was some hail, followed by a dreary, freezing rain. By the next day, Washington had developed a serious sore throat but "considering it as a trifling matter he took no measures to relieve it."[54] He did not, however, go out on his rounds that day. He remained busy around his house, walking outside to mark a few trees in the sloping yard that he wanted to have cut down. That night, his secretary advised him to take some medicine. Washington refused, stating, "You know I never take anything for a cold. Let it go as it came."[55]

But his sore throat did not leave him. Up in the night, he awoke Martha, complaining that he could barely speak and was having trouble breathing. For the next two days, Washington developed acute laryngitis, which turned into pleurisy, constricting his throat and threatening to suffocate him. He was bled four times, a common treatment of the day, but it only made him weaker. Martha remained at his side as doctors tended her husband. She wrapped his feet in a blanket to keep him warmer and begged that he not be bled any further. By four o'clock on the afternoon of December 14, he asked Martha to go downstairs and retrieve two wills from his desk. She did, he looked them both over, and ordered her to burn one of them. A little later he stated to his personal secretary, "I find I am going. My breath cannot continue long."[56]

Washington tried to speak several times as the sun sank below the horizon. But his words were faint and difficult to understand. He asked to be moved to a chair where he could sit near the fire, but he soon returned to his bed. After darkness had fallen, he spoke to one of his attending physicians: "Doctor, I die hard, but I am not afraid to go." Later in the evening, near 10 P.M., George Washington struggled to speak to one of his doctors the words that would be his last: "I am just going. Have me decently buried, and do not let my body be put into the vault in less than three days after I am dead. Do you understand me?" After his secretary said, "Yes, sir," Washington spoke one last time: "'Tis well." By midnight, struggling to breathe, Washington died. Martha was still at his side, and she asked calmly, "Is he gone?" Tobias

Washington's beloved Mount Vernon provides visitors with evidence of Washington's vision and his life as a country gentleman.

Lear, Washington's longtime secretary, said nothing, but held up his hand in answer.[57]

The people of the nation Washington helped establish mourned his death. Memorial services were held in various American cities for him. While many words were written to honor his passing, none are better remembered than those delivered by a fellow Virginian, Henry Lee. In his memorial address, one requested by Congress and spoken just two days after

Washington's death, Lee described the great general and political leader: "First in war, first in peace, first in the hearts of his countrymen."[58]

The history of the early United States is a story that cannot be told without including the life of George Washington. For more than 50 years, Washington's life helped define American history. From his days surveying the Virginia frontier to holding the highest office in the land, George Washington worked hard to establish a new country in a hostile world. Today, as more than two centuries ago, Washington remains an example of great leadership, both on the battlefield and in the halls of politics. Just as his sense of duty, of honor, of sacrificial service defined the man from Virginia, they continue to remind us why Washington will always be described as "The Father of Our Country."

Test Your Knowledge

I How many terms did Washington serve as president?

   a. One.

   b. Two.

   c. Three.

   d. Four.

2 What event sparked the Whiskey Rebellion?

   a. The tax on whiskey.

   b. An act making it illegal to produce whiskey privately.

   c. An attack on settlers in Whiskey, Pennsylvania.

   d. Dissatisfaction with Washington's policies toward France.

3 Who was Washington's successor as president?

   a. Thomas Jefferson.

   b. James Madison.

   c. James Monroe.

   d. John Adams.

4 In 1798, when John Adams asked Washington to lead the army in a possible war with France, how did Washington respond?

a. He refused, noting that the president should serve as commander-in-chief.

b. He refused, explaining that he was happy at Mount Vernon and did not want to leave.

c. He refused, disagreeing with the policies that had led the United States to the brink of war.

d. He agreed to serve.

5 Who described Washington as "first in war, first in peace, first in the hearts of his countrymen?"

a. Martha Washington.

b. John Adams.

c. Henry Lee.

d. Thomas Jefferson.

ANSWERS: 1. b; 2. a; 3. d; 4. d; 5. c

1732 George Washington is born in Virginia on February 22.

1743 Washington's father dies.

1748 Surveying expedition into the wilderness with George William Fairfax.

1749 Appointed Culpeper County surveyor.

1751 Travels to Barbados with half-brother Lawrence, who is sick with tuberculosis. While there, Washington contracts smallpox.

1752 Lawrence dies; Washington inherits Mount Vernon estate.

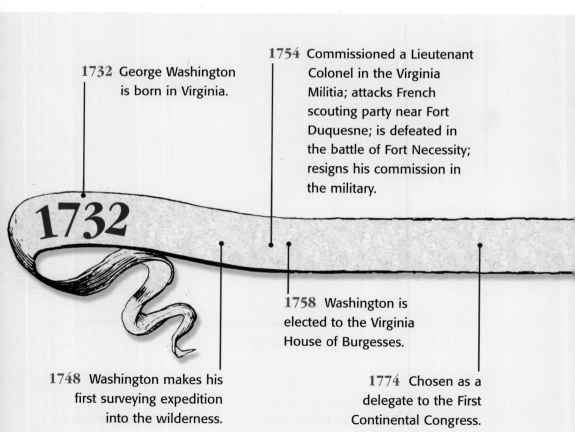

1732 George Washington is born in Virginia.

1754 Commissioned a Lieutenant Colonel in the Virginia Militia; attacks French scouting party near Fort Duquesne; is defeated in the battle of Fort Necessity; resigns his commission in the military.

1748 Washington makes his first surveying expedition into the wilderness.

1758 Washington is elected to the Virginia House of Burgesses.

1774 Chosen as a delegate to the First Continental Congress.

1753 Washington carries message to the French at Fort Le Boeuf.

1754 Commissioned a Lieutenant Colonel in the Virginia Militia; attacks French scouting party near Fort Duquesne; is defeated in the battle of Fort Necessity; resigns his commission in the military.

1755 Washington is appointed Colonel of all Virginia militia forces.

1758 Washington is elected to the Virginia House of Burgesses.

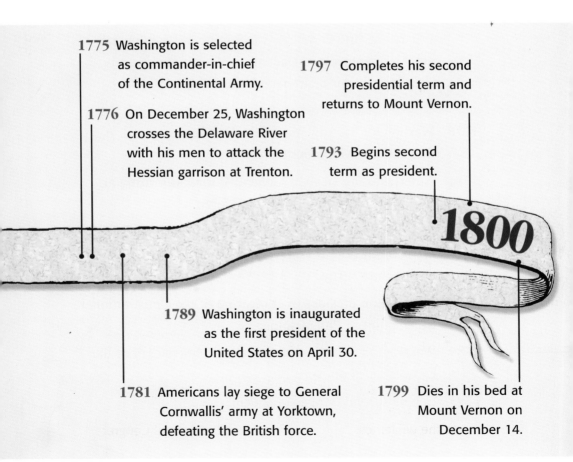

1775 Washington is selected as commander-in-chief of the Continental Army.

1776 On December 25, Washington crosses the Delaware River with his men to attack the Hessian garrison at Trenton.

1797 Completes his second presidential term and returns to Mount Vernon.

1793 Begins second term as president.

1800

1789 Washington is inaugurated as the first president of the United States on April 30.

1781 Americans lay siege to General Cornwallis' army at Yorktown, defeating the British force.

1799 Dies in his bed at Mount Vernon on December 14.

1759 Washington marries Martha Dandridge Custis.

1774 Chosen as a delegate to the First Continental Congress.

1775 Delegate to the Second Continental Congress; is selected as commander-in-chief of the Continental Army.

1776 Washington's army forces British to evacuate Boston; loses battles in New York City and is forced to evacuate. On December 25, Washington crosses the Delaware River with his men to attack the Hessian garrison at Trenton, New Jersey.

1777 Washington's men defeat the British in the battle of Princeton; British defeat Washington at Brandywine and Germantown; in December, Washington's army goes into winter quarters at Valley Forge, Pennsylvania.

1778 Washington's army attacks the British rear guard in the battle of Monmouth, New Jersey.

1781 Americans lay siege to General Cornwallis' army at Yorktown, defeating the British force.

1783 Peace Treaty of Paris is signed; Washington resigns his commission as commander-in-chief of the Continental Army.

1787 Washington presides over meeting of the Constitutional Convention in Philadelphia.

1789 Washington is inaugurated as the first president of the United States on April 30.

1793 Begins second term as president.

1797 Completes his second presidential term and returns to Mount Vernon.

1799 Dies in his bed at Mount Vernon on December 14.

Notes

CHAPTER 1
The Early Years
1. Quoted in David A. Adler, *George Washington: Father of Our Country* (New York: Holiday House, 1988), 10.

CHAPTER 2
Coming of Age
2. Quoted in Mario Rivoire, *The Life and Times of Washington* (Philadelphia: Curtis Publishing Company, 1965), 11.
3. Quoted in Ralph K. Andrist, ed., *George Washington: A Biography in His Own Words* (New York: Newsweek, 1972), 3.
4. Ibid., 4.
5. Ibid., 21.
6. Ibid.
7. Ibid., 24.

CHAPTER 3
Conflicts in the Wilderness
8. Ibid., 30.
9. Quoted in Marcus Cunliffe, *George Washington: Man and Monument* (London: St. James's Place, 1959), 42.
10. Ibid., 45.

CHAPTER 4
War on the Frontier
11. Quoted in Andrist, 52.
12. Quoted in Rivoire, 15.
13. Ibid.
14. Ibid., 57.
15. Quoted in *http://www.nps.gov/fon/braddock.htm.*

CHAPTER 5
The Coming of Revolution
16. Quoted in Cunliffe, 48.
17. Quoted in Rivoire, 62.
18. Ibid., 19.
19. Quoted in Andrist, 76.
20. Quoted in Cunliffe, 63.
21. Ibid.
22. Ibid.
23. Quoted in Andrist, 97-98.

CHAPTER 6
Commander in Chief
24. Quoted in Cunliffe, 65.
25. Quoted in Andrist, 100.
26. Quoted in Cunliffe, 67.
27. Quoted in James Thomas Flexner, *George Washington: The Forge of Experience (1732–1775)* (Boston: Little, Brown and Company, 1965), 131.
28. Ibid., 102.
29. Quoted in Rivoire, 33.
30. Ibid.
31. Ibid., 38.
32. Quoted in Cunliffe, 73.
33. Ibid.
34. Ibid., 74.
35. Quoted in Andrist, 152.
36. Ibid.

CHAPTER 7
Victory at Yorktown
37. Quoted in Cunliffe, 75.
38. Ibid.
39. Quoted in Rivoire, 53.

40. Ibid.
41. Quoted in Andrist, 170.
42. Quoted in Rivoire, 53.
43. Quoted in Cunliffe, 97.
44. Ibid.

CHAPTER 8
America's First President
45. Quoted in Rivoire, 58.
46. Quoted in George Washington, *Writings* (New York: The Library of America, 1991), 726.
47. Quoted in Tim McNeese, *The Revolutionary War* (St. Louis: Milliken Publishing, 2003), 33.
48. Quoted in Washington, 840.
49. Quoted in McNeese, *The Revolutionary War*, 37.

CHAPTER 9
A Final Farewell
50. Quoted in Washington, 977.
51. Quoted in Cunliffe, 146.
52. Ibid.
53. Quoted in Washington, 996.
54. Quoted in James Thomas Flexner, *Washington: The Indispensable Man* (Boston: Little, Brown and Company, 1974), 397.
55. Ibid.
56. Ibid., 400.
57. Ibid., 401.
58. Quoted in James Thomas Flexner, *George Washington: Anguish and Farewell (1793–1799)* (Boston: Little, Brown and Company, 1969), 502.

Andrist, Ralph K., ed. *George Washington: A Biography in His Own Words*. New York: Newsweek, 1972.

Collier, Christopher, and James Lincoln Collier. *The American Revolution, 1763–1783*. Tarrytown, N.Y.: Marshall Cavendish Corporation, 1988.

Cunliffe, Marcus. *George Washington: Man and Monument*. London: St. James's Place, 1959.

Ferling, John. *A Leap in the Dark: The Struggle to Create the American Republic*. New York: Oxford University Press, 2003.

Flexner, James Thomas. *George Washington: The Forge of Experience (1732–1775)*. Boston: Little, Brown and Company, 1965.

———. *George Washington: Anguish and Farewell (1793–1799)*. Boston: Little, Brown and Company, 1969.

———. *Washington: The Indispensable Man*. Boston: Little, Brown and Company, 1974.

Ketchum, Richard M. *The World of George Washington*. New York: American Heritage Publishing, 1974.

Lancaster, Bruce. *History of the American Revolution*. New York: Simon & Schuster, 2003.

McDowell, Bart. *The Revolutionary War: America's Fight For Freedom*. Washington, D.C.: National Geographic Society, 1983.

McNeese, Tim. *History in the Making: Sources and Essays of America's Past, Volume I*. New York: American Heritage, 1994.

———. *The Revolutionary War*. St. Louis: Milliken Publishing Company, 2003.

Rivoire, Mario. *The Life and Times of Washington*. Philadelphia: Curtis Publishing Company, 1965.

Tebbel, John. *George Washington's America*. New York: E.P. Dutton and Company, 1954.

Thane, Elswyth. *Potomac Squire*. New York: Meredith Press, 1963.

Washington, George. *Writings*. New York: The Library of America, 1991.

Further Reading

Adler, David A. *George Washington: Father of Our Country*. New York: Holiday House, 1988.

Ball, Elsie. *George Washington: First President*. New York: Abingdon Press, 1954.

Davis, Burke. *George Washington and the American Revolution*. New York: Random House, 1975.

Heilbroner, Joan. *Meet George Washington*. New York: Random House, 2001.

McClung, Robert M. *Young George Washington and the French and Indian War, 1753–1758*. North Haven, Conn.: Linnet Books, 2002.

Old, Wendie C. *George Washington*. Berkeley Heights, N.J.: Enslow Publishers, 1997.

Rosenburg, John M. *First in Peace: George Washington, the Constitution, and the Presidency*. Brookfield, Conn.: Millbrook Press, 1998.

Williams, Brian. *George Washington*. New York: Marshall Cavendish Corporation, 1988.

WEBSITES

George Washington: A National Treasure
www.georgewashington.si.edu

Library of Congress Profile of Washington
www.americaslibrary.gov/cgi-bin/page.cgi/aa/wash

Life of Washington
www.enchantedlearning.com/history/us/pres/washington

Mount Vernon
www.mountvernon.org

White House Biography of George Washington
www.whitehouse.gov/history/presidents/gw1.html

Index

page:

3: © Owaki-Kulla/CORBIS

10: © The Newark Museum/
Art Resource, NY

16: © Historical Picture Archive
/CORBIS

31: © CORBIS

40: © Bettmann/CORBIS

54: © Bettman/CORBIS

57: © CORBIS

70: © CORBIS

76: © Art Resource, NY

83: © Bettmann/CORBIS

87: © Bettmann/CORBIS

98: © Bettmann/CORBIS

100: © PoodlesRock/CORBIS

115: © Bettmann/CORBIS

122: © Bettmann/CORBIS

Cover: © National Portrait Gallery, Smithsonian Institution/Art Resource, NY

TIM McNEESE is a prolific author of books for elementary, middle school, high school, and college readers. He has published more than 70 books and educational materials over the past 20 years, on everything from Conestoga wagons to the French Revolution. Tim is an Associate Professor of History at York College in York, Nebraska. Previously, he taught middle and high school history, English, and journalism for 16 years. He is a graduate of York College, Harding University, and Southwest Missouri State University. His writing has earned him a citation in the library reference work *Something About the Author*. His wife, Beverly, is an Assistant Professor of English at York College. In 2003 and 2005, Tim and Beverly hosted a college study trip for students that followed 1,500 miles of the Lewis and Clark Trail. They have two children, Noah and Summer. Readers are encouraged to contact Professor McNeese at tdmcneese@york.edu.